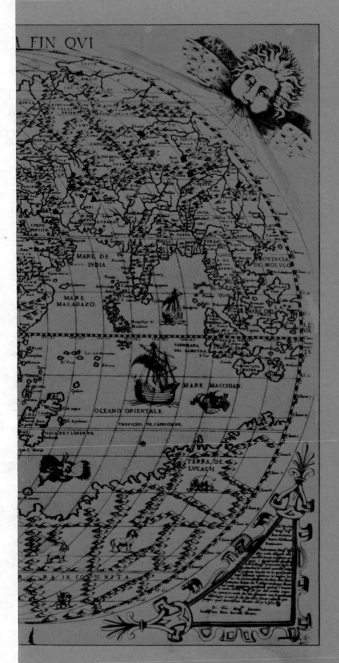

Planispher

c 1565, by Ferando

(front cover) *Shipping at Amsterdam,* by Abraham Storck (1644–c 1705). The large vessel on the left has the distinctive stern of the *fluyt.*

(back cover) *Shipping at an English port,* 1673, by Jacob Knyff (d. 1681). The port is imaginary but the beacon, ships and quayside are all well drawn. The *fluyt* is Dutch-built and represents one of the many captured in the Dutch Wars.

ACKNOWLEDGEMENTS

p.12 British Museum; pp.21,24,26 Master and Fellows of Magdalen College, Cambridge; pp.15–17 Museo Maritimo, Barcelona; p.40 Museo Navale, Madrid; p.11 Victoria and Albert Museum; p.48 Wasavarvet, Statens Sjohistoriska Museum, Stockholm; p.7 Mr Lionel Willis; remainder by courtesy of the Trustees of the National Maritime Museum.

ISBN 0 11 290313 4
Design by HMSO Graphic Design

Printed in England for
Her Majesty's Stationery Office
by Balding & Mansell, Wisbech, Cambs

Dd 696376   C150

National Maritime Museum

THE SHIP

Tiller and Whipstaff

The Development of the Sailing Ship

1400–1700

Alan McGowan

London
Her Majesty's Stationery Office

Contents

Fluyts getting under way in a light breeze, *c* 1665, Willem van de Velde (the Younger), 1633–1707. The rig of the *fluyt* is well drawn and the hull shape clearly shown in this picture. The drawing suggests that the mizzen of the *fluyt* on the left is a settee sail rather than a triangular lateen.

2

Introduction by the General Editor

This is the third of a series of ten short books on the development of the ship, both the merchant vessel and the specialised vessel of war, from the earliest times to the present day, commissioned and produced jointly by the National Maritime Museum and Her Majesty's Stationery Office.

The books are each self-contained, each dealing with one aspect of the subject, but together they cover the evolution of vessels in terms which are detailed, accurate and up-to-date. They incorporate the latest available information and the latest thinking on the subject, but they are readily intelligible to the non-specialist, professional historian or layman.

Above all, as should be expected from the only large and comprehensive general historical museum in the world which deals especially with the impact of the sea on the development of human culture and civilisation, the approach is unromantic and realistic. Merchant ships were and are machines for carrying cargo profitably. They carried the trade and, in the words of the very distinguished author of the second book of the series, 'The creation of wealth through trade is at the root of political and military power.' The vessel of war, the maritime vehicle of that power, follows, and she is a machine for men to fight from or with.

It follows from such an approach that the illustrations to this series are for the most part from contemporary sources. The reader can form his own conclusions from the evidence, written and visual. We have not commissioned hypothetical reconstructions, the annotation of which, done properly, would take up much of the text.

In this volume, Dr McGowan considers the history of the ship, both the merchant vessel and the ship of war, over the period between roughly the years 1400 and 1700. In so doing, he overlaps a little with the work of Dr McGrail in the first volume of this series in his account of the development of the non-edge-joined, skeleton-built three-masted ship. The production of this 'space capsule of the Renaissance' was not merely the most important single development to take place in the history of the ship until compound and triple expansion steam engines were brought to the point of regular commercial use in the middle of the second half of the nineteenth century, it was one of the most important developments of its kind in human history.

At present we know remarkably little about it. Now that the double development has been identified, recognised and accepted, and its significance begun to be appreciated, we may hope that the evidence will be sought out and examined more thoroughly than in the past. Work of this kind began at the National Maritime Museum three years ago and at the time of writing (1980) has made sufficient progress to justify a report in the not very distant future. But this will only be the beginning of the proper study which must take place in several countries and languages over a long period of time.

Meanwhile, Dr McGowan wisely does no more than indicate some of the evidence in his first chapter and draws no conclusions. The rest of his book considers the development of the ship after things have more or less settled down from the revolutionary developments of the early and middle 1400s. This produced by 1700 reasonably efficient specialised merchant vessels capable of carrying cargoes to many different parts of the world profitably while the fighting ship developed to a point of efficiency not far short of the final form of the sailing vessel of war.

Dr McGowan is the Head of the Department of Ships in the National Maritime Museum.

Basil Greenhill
DIRECTOR, NATIONAL MARITIME MUSEUM
General Editor

Preface

The three centuries from 1400 to 1700 saw two great technological developments. The first and more important was the development of the three-masted ship, arguably the most significant piece of technology created by man since the making of fire and use of the wheel. The three-masted ship made possible voyages to the Indies, opening a trade route that was not dependent upon the goodwill of the peoples of the Eastern Mediterranean. Even more important it made possible the discovery by Europeans of the vast continent of the New World.

If the second development was of less consequence in terms of world history it was still of major importance in terms of politics and trade, two of the means by which the world and its society grows. The first technological development had produced the three-masted ship out of the one- and two-masted late medieval vessels of the Baltic, North Sea and Atlantic coast and the Mediterranean. The second development took the simple three-masted ship and produced the 100-gun First Rate of the mid-17th century, a vessel of sufficient force that it would have been a welcome addition to either side at the Battle of Trafalgar, more than 150 years later. At the same time a parallel evolution was taking place in merchant vessels. Specialist cargo-carrying ships were introduced with a quite different ethos. Their function was measured not so much in power and sailing qualities as by the economical rate at which they could carry the most cargo with the least running costs and therefore at the lowest price. In 1500, in most cases, warships and merchants ships of the same size were indistinguishable. Two hundred years later, at the end of our period, they were rarely so. This is a measure of the success with which they had been developed for the specialised requirements of their trade.

This work is of necessity, largely a synthesis of the research of others which I hope has properly been acknowledged in general in the list of works consulted, if not always in particular. The conclusions however are my own unless specifically acknowledged.

The Three-masted Ship

Ultimately all forms of transport evolve under the influence of economic factors. Frequently the result of direct causes, the evolution is often also a result of indirect economic influence as in the case of a specific wartime development, for wars, especially maritime wars, are often fought for economic reasons. This influence of trade upon the evolution of transport is particularly demonstrable in ships, as this series of books shows, and the most profound manifestation of that influence occurred in the early years of the 15th century.

As a result, not only was man's knowledge of the physical world enlarged almost beyond his comprehension, but also the political and economic balance was altered and the course of history changed. Literally, the world was never to be the same again.

At the end of the 14th century, the world as it was known to Western civilisation was centred on the Mediterranean Sea. To the north its extremities lay in what must have seemed the wintry Scandinavian landscapes – and the far off island of Iceland. To the Mediterranean peoples the islands of Britain were only marginally less remote.

The western horizon of this world lay a hundred miles or so out in the Atlantic Ocean; to the south the arid wastes of the North African deserts inhibited exploration by land. The seas off the Atlantic coast of Morocco seemed to offer a worthwhile route but while persistent northerly winds and a current set to the southward were tempting aids, the difficulty of returning against them was daunting. When the wind dropped there was frequently fog and, perhaps worst of all, the coastal waters abounded in shallows. At the other end of North Africa the great sea to the south-east, by whose coasts Marco Polo had returned, was well known but few Europeans had seen it and no European vessel had sailed upon it. The only known route out of this world dominated by the Mediterranean was across the vast plains of Asia to the fabled lands of the East, but the trade routes were dominated by a combination of the problems of distance, difficult terrain and frequently by the war-like peoples of the lands through which they passed.

To reach beyond the confines of this world, to explore the far western waters of the Atlantic Ocean or to sail southward along the coast of Africa until, it was hoped, the southernmost cape could be rounded and the great eastern sea entered would require a very special ship, one towards which, probably without realising it, the seamen of the day were already reaching. The new form of vessel had to be special in two very important ways: first it had to be able physically to carry the explorer and his crew together with enough supplies to last throughout many weeks of sailing; second, but no less important, it had to give them confidence that it would be sufficient for their needs.

The new vessel was the three-masted ship. But it was not the three-masted ship merely because three masts and the form of hull construction used permitted the building of a larger vessel than hitherto. On the contrary, a leading authority, Señor Martinez-Hidalgo, has calculated that the *Santa Maria* (see p.16), *c* 1492, was approximately the same length (77 ft) as the Bremen cog (see p.7), *c* 1400, although admittedly she was 2 ft 6 ins more in the beam (25 ft 6 ins). Both the *Santa Maria's* consorts, *Niña* and *Pinta* were smaller. In the event the three-masted ship was used because that was the vessel that gave the explorer confidence. Important though the rig was, however, that was only one of the two highly critical factors involved. The other was the form of construction of the hull.

In the countries bordering the seas of Northern Europe a boatbuilding tradition had developed over several hundred years: the edge-joined construction using overlapping planks, known as clinker-building. This form of construction is discussed in detail by Seán McGrail in the first volume of this series.

By the 14th century this method had been adapted to different uses. One important type of vessel that had evolved was the cog, a flat-bottomed, capacious cargo ship developed in the 12th century, perhaps for, and certainly adopted for use by, the Hanseatic League. The cog was often built without a keel, at other times with a simple keel-plank, from which the stem and stern posts rose sharply and in a straight line. The bottom planking was laid flush, *i.e.* edge to edge, the steep, high sides being clinker-built from the turn of the bilge.

For centuries our only knowledge of the cog came from documentary evidence and from drawings of variable quality and in an often unsympathetic media. At least one such illustration, however, that on the seal of the Hanse town of Elbing *c* 1350, was shown to be surprisingly accurate when the greater part of the hull of a cog, dating from about 1400, was recovered from the mud of Bremen harbour in 1962 (see p.7).

The cog dominated the northern carrying trade, particularly that from the Baltic, salt fish (especially herring), leather, hides, grain and wool, as well as the naval stores of timber, pitch, tar and turpentine, for about 150 years. Towards the end of the 14th century the records suggest that the cog was displaced by the hulc as the chief carrier of bulk goods in northern waters. Like the cog it seems to have been single-masted but it was presumably larger. It is fortunate that the hulc had a relatively short life as the major carrier, for we know far less about the hulc than the cog, the best representations appearing on the font in Winchester Cathedral, on the seal of West Shoreham, and on coins from the site of the Palace of Placentia in the centre of the grounds of the Royal Naval College at Greenwich. We know little about the construction of the hulc but it was almost certainly a variation of the clinker tradition.

This shell construction, in which frames were inserted after the skin or shell of planking had been completed, relied for much of its strength upon the overlapped edge-fastenings. As these did not increase in strength by the same proportion in which the timber became heavier, there was a limit to the size of vessel that could be built. One of the largest vessels built in this way was Henry V's *Grâce Dieu* (1416) which was almost as long as the *Victory*. Clinker-built warships—although they were probably little different in construction from merchant ships of a similar size—continued until the early 16th century when, to maintain stability with the carriage of heavier guns, ordnance had to be mounted on a lower deck with holes or gun ports cut in the side of the ship to enable the guns to fire. As ports cut through edge-joined planking would weaken the basic structure to an unacceptable extent, a different method of building—skeleton construction—had to be employed.

On the Atlantic coasts and in northern waters the hulc was replaced by what has become known as the carrack. This term is associated with unnamed ships depicted in a number of 14th and 15th century illustrations because of their similarity with the well-known drawing labelled a *kraeck*, by the Flemish artist who signed it with a W followed by a symbol that looks rather like a letter A (see p.12). Because of that, historians have also termed carracks the ships developed out of the influence of the two building traditions, although there seems to be no evidence that the name was actually applied to them at the time. It is to these carracks that we now turn.

The major impact of the cog in the development of ships in the Mediterranean seems to have been in the depth and breadth of the hull and the convenience and power, under certain conditions, of the square sail. The shape of the hull enabled the carriage of a large and bulky cargo, while its height also made it more difficult for attackers to board, no small consideration at a time when piracy was a common hazard at sea. Understandably, the Mediterranean builders preferred to construct this new hull in the skeleton method they commonly used. Instead of the

The Bremen cog, c 1400. Recovered from the harbour at Bremen, the cog is 77 ft in length and 23 ft in the beam. She shows all the characteristics of the cog: high sides, with a straight but angled stem and stern post. The cog is now on display in the Maritime Museum at Bremerhaven.

straight stem and sternpost of the cog, which gave a long, straight, flat bottom, they also preferred a curved stem running back into the keel, which had the effect of enabling the hull to turn more quickly.

Into this hull were stepped two masts, but at this point we have two different vessels emerging, distinguished by the position of the masts and the type of sail used. In the most numerous of these two forms, the vessel had a main mast square-rigged with a single sail, and a lateen sail on a small mizzen mast. If we accept that this was a Mediterranean development, this is the way the rig might be expected to develop: to the square mainsail associated with the broad deep hull, the Mediterranean seaman would have added the sail he understood best, the lateen. Its purpose was twofold: to assist in steering and to make more ground to windward.

In the second of these two-masted types, the masts were fore and main, each with a square sail. Theoretically this was a far less efficient rig; nevertheless it is interesting that it was tried and indeed persisted with long enough to have been considered sufficiently common to record.

Before going on to look at the final stage of the evolution of the three-masted ship in the second half of the 15th century, it should be remembered that in this brief survey we are looking at types that were pushing at the frontiers of development. In the northern waters there were also numerous types of one-masted vessel akin to or quite different from the cog. A certain amount is known of these vessels, particularly the Dutch and the English as we will see later, but little in detail. They were all, we may be virtually certain, built in the clinker tradition. In the Mediterranean the vast majority of vessels were still lateen rigged and all, it seems, were by now skeleton-built, i.e. had a pre-constructed skeleton of frames to which the planking was then fastened. The planks were flush-laid and not edge-joined. In those published shipbuilding contracts for the 14th century which have been examined, there is no suggestion that anything other than a form of skeleton construction was in use in the Mediterranean in this period.

It may also be useful to consider briefly the nature of the wooden structure which made up the hull of ships with which both this volume and the next in the series are concerned, as well as to the principal types of sail.

First, the structure. A wooden ship was pliable and this basic characteristic applied in a great or lesser degree to all wooden sailing ships, not only during the five and a half centuries that have elapsed since the three-masted ship appeared, but also during the 5000 years preceding it, whether vessels were built of shell, edge-joined construction or by skeleton construction. Ships were built of wood, of a vast number of pieces of wood in fact, fastened together with large nails, still larger iron bolts driven through pre-drilled holes and clenched over the tip, and large wooden pegs (usually of oak). For much of this long span of the sailing ship's life, certainly throughout our period and subsequently into the 20th century, the sails were made from flax or cotton canvas suspended from wooden masts and yards supported by the natural fibre rigging, usually made from hemp. Structurally, both wood and hemp are relatively springy materials, so masts and rigging continually 'worked' under the changing loads exerted by the wind. Wooden hulls were also deflected under the variable loads of the wind, of the buoyancy of water and waves, of the ship's own weight and its cargo or armament and, in heavy seas, of the violent impact from waves. Because of the inherent springiness of wood, and also because a wooden hull was necessarily made up of thousands of individual pieces joined together, a certain degree of flexibility was unavoidable.

Flexibility in sailing vessels was indeed held by many seamen to be of positive value. They believed that it allowed a vessel to ride the waves more easily and so, by 'giving' to seas, to absorb their force better. There is evidence that pirates and privateers removed certain heavy knees in order to make their craft lighter and more flexible. Flexible vessels were also held by some to be faster because they were free to ride with the seas instead of battering through them. However, though such ideas may have been firmly held, they have not been validated by any modern theories on ship dynamics.

We have spoken already of square sails and lateen sails and it may be useful to understand something of the characteristics and attributes of each. These qualities apply in sailing today and differ from those of the 15th century only in degree.

A square sail is set from a yard suspended from the forward side of a mast and receives the wind on one side only. Although its angle may be changed to receive the wind more squarely on the after surface, it always remains with its centre above the centre-line of the vessel. This type of sail was developed in the northern seas where winds of gale force are common and frequently last for days on end. Under such conditions it is important that as much of the wind's force as possible should be applied to the ship over its centre-line.

The Mediterranean conditions, as might be supposed, affected the rig of vessels used in them no less than did the stormy weather of the northern seas. In the Mediterranean Sea, the lighter and more variable winds allowed advantageous use of the lateen sail. This fore-and-aft sail was set from a long lateen yard suspended at an angle on the leeward side of the mast. It could receive the wind on either side. The great virtue of the fore-and-aft sail is that it enables a vessel to be sailed much closer to the wind than would be possible with only a square sail. Clumsy by

modern standards though the lateen sail was, it had all the advantages for going to windward.

The importance of a ship's being able to sail well to windward, *i.e.* as nearly as possible in the direction from which the wind is coming, cannot be over-stressed, as it gave the master a wider range of options in choosing his course. In a warship the ability to get to windward of the enemy would often enable a commander to dictate the course of action; at least it gave him the option of accepting or refusing action. For the master of a merchant ship it could mean making a tide – and so port – or not; on a lee shore for either merchant or warship it could make the difference between safety and disaster, life or death. For merchant ships in particular, which unlike warships, were not built with fine lines to achieve the best sailing qualities, it was generally not convenient or economically sound practice to accept long passages to windward. The common practice was to lay a course that would bring long periods with the wind abaft the beam. The disadvantage of a few extra days sailing was outweighed by the reduced wear and tear on gear. Much of course depended upon the ships themselves, as will be seen later in discussing the route taken to the Cape of Good Hope by the Portuguese in the late 15th century.

The lateen sail had its disadvantages, however. When changing to another tack, the yard had to be swung almost vertical in order that it could be reset on the lee side of the mast. This was no easy task in heavy weather even though, under storm conditions, a small lateen with its own light yard was usually set. Further, with the lateen sail spread wide when running *i.e.* with the wind almost directly aft, there was a danger that in heavily gusting winds the leverage so far out from the vessel's centre of gravity would cause it to capsize.

There is so little real evidence that we may never know when these virtues of hull and rig were first combined to make the three-masted ship, or by whom. It seems probable that it was the seamen of Genoa, for they not only had the skill and experience, but they also had the incentive. Their trade, as we have seen, was essentially in bulk goods with a high stowage factor, such as grain, alum, or wool, where the cargo had to be large before it was of great value. The three-masted ship may have been the product of the Venetians, who also had the necessary skill and experience in northern waters; but Venice controlled the trade with the Indies, the luxury trade in spices, expensive fabrics such as silk and satin, and precious stones. Although Venetian merchants were also in the other trades—indeed any trade where there was a profit to be made—the incentive to experiment and, above all, to lay out considerable capital sums on a new and more expensive type of ship may have been lacking. It is possible that the three-masted ship was the product of Spanish or even Portuguese seamen, but the trade of the Iberian peninsula was not to be compared with that of Genoa and perhaps, therefore, they also had less incentive. We don't know.

At all events this new vessel, the three-masted ship, seems to have appeared in the first quarter of the 15th century. The Spanish and Portuguese refer to the *nao*, the Italians to the *nave* whilst, as we have seen, the northern nations have called it the carrack. Terminology is extremely difficult, for *nave* and *nao* were general terms just as we use 'vessel' or 'ship' today. 'Carrack' referred to a particular type of vessel in the 16th century but again, as we have seen, for the 15th century its use stems solely from the caption on a drawing by an unknown, if accomplished, Flemish artist.

The basis of the three-masted ship was a broad beam and deep hull, necessary both to withstand the battering of northern seas and to carry a large volume of cargo, two characteristics of the cog and the hulk. The proportions were commonly 1:2:3 in beam, length of keel and length on the deck. The hull was skeleton-built with a curved stem and perhaps at first a curved stern-post.

The driving power came from the square sail on the main mast. Its lowest part, approximately a quarter of the whole, comprised the bonnet which was a separate section of the sail laced along its upper edge to the upper part. In heavy weather, the bonnet could be quickly stripped off to reduce the area of sail set. Later, as mainsails grew larger the bonnet was laced on in two parts, the upper retaining the name bonnet, the part laced to it in turn being called, in Britain at least, the drabler. The mainmast itself consisted of a number of lengths of mast timber shaped on the inside to fit together to create the necessary thickness to withstand the strains placed upon it. The pieces were held together by woldings (rope binding) every few feet.

Initially, the fore and mizzen sails were mainly aids to steering, providing leverage at the extremities of the vessels. When one considers that all vessels of this period, regardless of size, had to be steered by a tiller controlled by tackles in all but the lightest of breezes, the importance of achieving some form of balance in the sail plan becomes immediately apparent.

The mizzen mast was a single stick which could be stepped on the keel as it had to be placed far enough forward to allow for the arc of the tiller. Because of this it could be fairly substantial, no doubt one of the reasons why the lateen sail became quite large—larger than would be required for a mere steering sail—at an early date.

The foremast however, needing to be set as far forward as possible to achieve the maximum effect, had to be stepped on a deck beam below the fore-castle because of the curve of the stem. As a consequence it could only be a light single spar, and bore a small square sail.

The masts were supported by stays and shrouds which were tightened by the use of dead-eyes and lanyards. At this period the shrouds seem to have been secured inboard. At the head of the main mast was a railed platform or top, a valuable vantage point for a look-out or, in a fight, bowmen. The top was reached by a vertical ladder attached to the mast as the shrouds were rigged in the Mediterranean fashion of the time, without ratlines.

The yards differed as did the masts. The small yard for the foresail was invariably a single spar. The main yard was nearly always constructed by fishing two spars together. The lateen yard seems to have varied: occasionally a single spar, sometimes a fished spar. The reason for this seems to have been simple economics. Although there were pine forests adjacent to the Mediterranean, particularly on the Dalmatian coast, good mast timber was not as readily available as it was to countries close to the Baltic Sea. Northern mast timber would have been very expensive and, in the Mediterranean experience, had not been found necessary, for the very long lateen yards used on the

Three-masted ship, *c* 1425. This Hispano–Moorish bowl at the Victoria and Albert Museum shows a three-masted ship not unlike that of *c* 1480 shown in the illustration on p.14. The hull shows the same characteristics; for the rig, the lateen mizzen sail is set and the bonnet is clearly shown on the mainsail. One of the most interesting features is the spritsail which is plainly rigged below the bowsprit. This is the earliest illustration of this yard and sail, which if the dating of this piece is accurate (see acknowledgments) shows the square spritsail in use some 30–40 years earlier than has previously been supposed.

galleys were always fished – and continued to be so as long as such vessels lasted. Even as late as the 19th century, lateen yards in use on Mediterranean vessels were fished, so there was, no doubt, a strong element of tradition behind using a fished long main yard. The longest lateen yards were probably lighter in weight than the main yard of even the early carracks but the fished main yard appears well into the 16th century.

One of the earliest illustrations of a three-masted ship appears on a bowl for long identified as having come from southern Spain in the second quarter of the 15th century (see p.11) but which it now seems may be earlier than 1425. The drawing contains an intriguing blend of sophisticated detail and *gaucherie*, the latter surprising in view of the competence of the work generally, and not in any way due to the constraints of the medium.

During the 15th century the carrack increased in size, but equally important, the rig was developed. The innovations did not include anything as radical as the addition of the fore and mizzen masts had been, but they were significant.

England was by no means the foremost nation in trading by sea in the 15th century and yet records of merchant ships hired by the crown indicate that by mid-century the largest vessels had nearly doubled in size since 1422. In addition and as might be expected, the larger ships of 200 tons burden and above comprised a greater proportion of the merchant fleet. For 105 vessels hired by the Crown in the period 1399–1422, the average was 81 tons burden; for 161 hired in the years 1449–1451, it was 117 tons. Naturally one must be wary of reading too much into limited statistics, but trends can certainly be traced in this way. The trend in question, the increase in size, is confirmed by an examination of the ships, both English and foreign, for which trade licences or safe conducts during the wars with France were issued in the two periods 1461–1467 and 1472–1483. For the 61 English ships listed, the average is 159 tons, and whereas in the first two periods (1399–1422 and 1449–1451) ships of 240 tons and more number one and 11 respectively, in the third list (1461–1467 and 1472–1483) there are 15. For the foreign vessels, largely French (222 ships) and Spanish (111 ships), the average is 141 tons. This lower average than for the English ships is explained by the large number of French vessels smaller than 100 tons employed in the cross-channel trade. Although only 26 of the 342

Kraeck, c 1470. One of a series of drawings by the Flemish artist who signed his work with a W followed by a symbol rather like an A, this is the most detailed illustration known of a 15th century three-masted ship.

foreign vessels listed are of 240 tons or more, compared with 15 out of the 61 English ships listed, some of the larger vessels are very large indeed with one of 600 tons, one of 700 tons, four of 800 tons and one of 1000 tons.

During this period when the size of ships was increasing – roughly 1450–1485 – illustrations suggest that the sails were also made larger. This is evident in both the foresail and the lateen mizzen, but particularly the latter. Whilst still carrying out their original function as balancing and steering sails, they were also utilised increasingly as driving sails, and the lateen mizzen had reached a size where it could contribute considerable effort in sailing to windward. The most famous depiction of an early carrack dates from this period, the drawing of a *kraeck* (*c* 1470) by a Flemish master (p.12). Although rather exaggerated in the drawing perhaps, it is clear that the lateen sail was much larger than a mere steering sail need have been. The foresail too is depicted as being of considerable size although not overdrawn. An interesting rigging detail shows the shrouds fastened through chainwales (channels) outside the hull in order to widen the angle and afford more support for the masts. This drawing is the first showing so much detail of rigging, all of which is understandable to the modern sailor, and which suggests therefore that W., the Flemish master, was closely familiar with his subject.

A significant feature of the *kraeck* drawing is the amount of top hamper shown, in the form of the fore and aftercastles. Not only are there two forecastle decks but also above them is an awning framework, all of which must have produced considerable windage even without the awning rigged. The aftercastle is similarly built up and together the two castles seem to set enormous problems, suggesting a drift to leeward that even the large lateen sail would have difficulty in counteracting. Whatever problems they

caused, however, the lofty fore and aftercastles became characteristic of the carrack from then onward.

At about the same time as this development occurred – or perhaps soon after – the rig was extended a stage further: the introduction, almost simultaneously, of the spritsail and the main topsail. The appearance of these two new sails, at the same time, is unlikely to be a coincidence. No one has left any written record of why they were introduced; again the evidence is circumstantial, but convincing enough. One thing is certain: there was a reason for their development. No owner, master or seaman ever rigged an additional sail, with all the extra cost and labour involved, without the likelihood of its being beneficial in one way or another.

The addition of high castles at both bow and stern would not in themselves have upset the balance of the vessel. The main effect of the increased windage would cause the vessel to drift bodily to leeward and in order to counteract this drift and make more ground to windward it seems possible that the lateen mizzen was made larger relative to the increase in size of the foresail. It may be that this imbalance occurred independently of the building up of the castles because of the limits placed on the foremast and foresail. The fact remains, however, that these changes in rig and the addition of considerable top-hamper were more or less concurrent.

This new imbalance in the sail plan was put right by the introduction of the spritsail, a square sail set from a yard slung on the underside of the bowsprit. Because of its position, actually forward of the bows of the vessel, this quite small sail could exert a leverage far beyond what might be expected from its size, and being small it could be handled quite easily.

At roughly the same time, that is in the 25 years *c* 1450–1475, the main topsail was introduced. In addition to the mere fact of increasing the driving power, the topsail brought with it three advantages,

Three-masted ship *c* 1480. This drawing by an unknown artist is one of the earliest depictions of a three-masted ship in which interpretation is not complicated by the medium. The square sails have their foot pulled in to the mast, a feature of mid-15th century rigging. This is the earliest known illustration of a topsail and must represent a very brief evolutionary stage. It is understandable that early experimental topsails would be quite small and that the problem of what to do with the tacks of a square topsail was not immediately solved. The triangular topsail was an obvious step in view of the way in which the foot of the square sails was secured to the mast. It became apparent however that the topmast could carry a much larger, wider sail, the tacks of which, if it were quadrilateral, could be conveniently secured to the main yard.

one of which is directly associated with the spritsail. We do not know whether the seamen of the day were conscious of the virtues of the topsail when it was introduced, although it would be presumptuous to assume too readily that they were not aware of them.

As well as simply providing more power then, the topsail was first, under certain conditions of light and fitful breezes, able to produce more continuous power than the mainsail. In a swell, or choppy sea, the breeze is often likely to be more constant 40–50 feet above sea level than lower down. Second, although this may have had little relevance until topmasts were sturdier, it could provide enough power to keep the ship steady when even the reefed mainsail (in our period, a mainsail reduced by having the bonnet or bonnets stripped off) was too much. Third, the topsail was a lifting sail, that is, it lifted the bows slightly, so easing the passage of the hull through the water. Now, whilst this was an asset at any time, it was particularly useful to counter one of the less favourable effects of the spritsail. Under certain conditions, when running or with the wind on the quarter, the spritsail could have the disturbing effect of pulling the bows lower into the water, so reducing speed and impairing the very manoeuvreability the sail was set to impart. The main topsail had the effect of nullifying this tendency which makes its introduction, at much the same time as the spritsail, understandable. We cannot be sure whether the topmast on which this sail was set was a continuation of the lower mast, *i.e.* a pole-mast, or whether, as seems more probable, it was a separate but fixed topmast. There is reasonable evidence to suggest that the topmast that could be lowered was not introduced until late in the 16th century. The illustration above, dated *c* 1480, at the end of this 25–30 year period when these particular innovations appeared, strongly suggests a separate topmast although no doublings are shown.

With these developments the three-masted ship, while by no means yet developed to its peak, had evolved to the state where it was a convenient and proper vehicle for the trans-oceanic explorations and the trade that would inevitably follow them. In all essentials it was complete, the changes made during the subsequent 350 years and seen when the three-masted square-rigged wooden ship was at its zenith technologically being refinements rather than innovation: a more weatherly hull, a more complex and complete sail plan – always with balance in mind – and the introduction in the 18th century of an increasing proportion of fore and aft sails, following the lead of the lateen mizzen, to improve the sailing qualities to windward.

The most important consequence of the three-masted ship was the discovery of the New World, in the last years of the 15th century. But another important type of vessel, the caravel, was also used by Columbus on his four voyages to the West (1492–1504). Even more important perhaps, it had earlier proved the means by which the difficulties of exploring southwards along the Atlantic coast of Africa had been overcome.

The caravel was not a 'new' vessel in the same sense as the three-masted ship, but very little is known about its development. References in 13th century manuscripts suggest that it was originally a fishing boat, probably without a deck, and rigged with a lateen sail. During the 14th century, perhaps, it was enlarged, fitted with a deck and given two masts. It is just possible that this transformation was less a process of natural evolution than one of a positive decision made under the influence of Prince Henry the Navigator, who was determined to explore as fully as possible the west coast of Africa.

By 1420 the Madeira Islands and the Canary Islands were well known but repeated efforts to round Cape Bojador failed until 1433. Cape Bojador,

Caravel *Niña*, 1492. Columbus' favourite of all his ships, the lateen-rigged *Niña* was converted to square-rig (cf. *Pinta* p.16) in the Canary Islands on the first voyage. The light construction and weatherly lines of the caravel are apparent in both models.

in a latitude of 26° 20′ north, juts out some 25 miles to the westward from the mainland. There are widespread and dangerous shallows made worse by the northerly gales; the current is strong and constantly to the southward and when the prevailing winds drop there is frequently thick fog; the coast is barren and uninviting. These conditions are sufficient to make any modern navigator of a small boat pause. In the 15th century, with the menacing background of the legends of the Green Sea of Darkness from which, popular superstition had it, there was no return, they were terrifying; and with both current and prevailing wind pushing to the south there was some justification in the popular belief. Only a vessel capable of making good ground to windward stood any chance of return – and this of course, is where the caravel came in. The fact that it took more than ten years to double Cape Bojador seems to lend credence to the suggestion that the caravel of the great explorations was developed quite deliberately.

By estimation based on the work of José Maria Martinez-Hidalgo the caravel was about 50–60 feet long overall with a beam of about 18 feet. The hull was fairly low in profile (see p.15), without any of the superstructure which was at that time becoming characteristic in the carrack, and it was of skeleton construction. The rig was entirely fore and aft, both

Square-rigged caravel *Pinta*, 1492. Caravels were originally lateen-rigged with either two masts or three. The fact that the *Pinta* had already been converted to square rig before being selected for the great voyage of Columbus shows how experience in Atlantic waters was already affecting ideas of rig. This modern reconstruction and that of the *Nina* were built under the direction of Señor Martinez-Hidalgo, Director of the Museo Maritime, Barcelona.

masts being lateen rigged. The interesting thing is that two-masted lateeners in the Mediterranean seem generally to have had a fore and main mast. The caravel had a main mast and a mizzen mast.

It was at all events a combination of hull and rig that proved extremely successful in the very difficult coastal navigation that was required. Within ten years of rounding Cape Bojador, the Portuguese explorers had also rounded Cape Verde, leaving behind the desert coast, to find themselves in a most fertile region with promise and prospects of trade. Even the rounding of the Cape of Good Hope nearly 3500 miles to the south was thereafter only a matter of time, a feat achieved inadvertently by Bartholomew Diaz in a storm in 1487.

These feats of exploration combined to impel a Genoese seaman, Christopher Columbus, to try to find a route to the Indies by sailing westward into the Atlantic in 1492. His three ships were the *Santa Maria*, a carrack, and two caravels, the *Niña* and the *Pinta*. The *Pinta* had already been converted to square rig when she was purchased, and the *Niña* was re-rigged in the Canary Islands because he intended to use the steady, prevailing winds of the north-east trades on the way out and the equally steady westerlies on the way back.

The *Santa Maria* was rigged with spritsail, foresail, mainsail and main topsail and lateen mizzen. The *Pinta* had a square foresail, a mainsail and a lateen mizzen; the *Niña*, originally lateen rigged on both masts – main and mizzen – was re-rigged in a manner similar to the *Pinta*.

Suffice to say, in concluding this story of the three-masted ship, that although Columbus announced himself fully satisfied with the sufficiency of his vessels before he sailed, and although he was later critical of the *Santa Maria* and was full of praise for the *Niña*, it was the three-masted ship that made the voyage possible. The *Santa Maria* was criticised as having too deep a draught and for being unweatherly, for she could at best sail nine points – $101\frac{1}{4}°$ – off the wind. The caravels, on the other hand, were built to sail five points – $56\frac{1}{4}°$ – off the wind. It is almost certain that the *Niña* could not sail as close as that once she had been converted to square rig (*caravela redonda*) but with her fine lines she could perhaps have made six and a half to seven points as a three-masted ship and it was as a three-masted ship that the *Niña* was judged. It is intriguing to reflect that the actual physical properties of the three-masted ship were probably not, in the event, an essential requirement for the great explorations of the 15th century, although it was most important for the great ships of both trade and war that followed. The voyage of Columbus in fact might even have been made in a

Santa Maria. These plans were drawn in 1963 by Señor Martinez-Hidalgo for the reconstruction of a model of the *Santa Maria*; they have been redrawn for this illustration.

well-found cog, which would have been perfectly capable of using, profitably enough, the north-east trade winds on the outward leg and the westerlies on the way home, although it might be argued that the hull form and construction of a cog would not have withstood long periods of heavy weather. This brings us back to the earlier statement, that the three-masted ship was necessary really in that it gave the explorers confidence. It was seamanlike – as well as ordinary common sense – for Columbus to demand that his vessels should be able to operate under the most varied and unexpected conditions. This the cog could not do but the *Santa Maria* and the converted caravels could; and to this extent, the three-masted ship was an essential prerequisite to the great ocean discoveries of the 15th century.

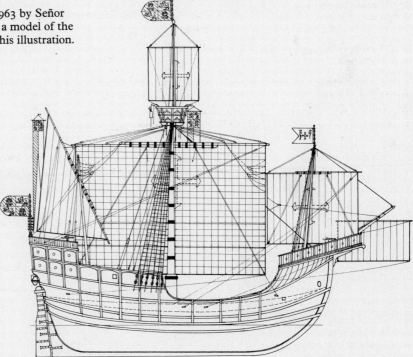

Carrack and Galleon

Columbus's criticism of the carrack—for so the northern seamen would perhaps have described the *Santa Maria*—was directed naturally at its capabilities as a vessel for exploration. Once the route had been established, far bigger ships were required to enable Spain to exploit the possibilities of the new lands. The Portuguese had already reached the same conclusions concerning their trade with the East.

Nearly ten years separated the rounding of the Cape of Good Hope by Bartholomew Diaz and Vasco da Gama's voyage to India. Although the internal political and economic affairs of Portugal have been blamed for this delay, there seems to be much to commend Professor C.R.Boxer's view expressed in *The Portuguese Seaborne Empire* that once the Portuguese knew that the voyage was a certainty (*i.e.* after Diaz in 1487-1488) they spent time looking for an easier route. Diaz and his predecessors had been forced to battle against the contrary south-easterly trade winds because they were sailing in unknown waters and needed to stay within touch of the land. Their object, after all, was to round Africa. Once the latitude of the Cape had been established they could search for an easier way of getting there. This easier route was important because the great *naos*, the square-rigged ships with the cargo carrying capacity necessary for profitable trade, could not be certain of reaching the Cape of Good Hope against the unfavourable trade winds and the northward flowing Benguella Current. The caravels on the other hand had not the cargo space, although they had the requisite sailing qualities.

It seems probable that by the time da Gama sailed, the new route had been well reconnoitred and that da Gama himself used it in 1497. Certainly it was the route taken by the Portuguese merchants of the 16th and 17th centuries. They sailed southward on the north-east trades, then through the doldrums to pick up the south-east trades, crossing the equator to the south of Cape Verde somewhere in the region of what we would now call the longitude of 20° west. Using the south-east trade winds they then made their way south-westwards until the Brazil Current took them southward to pick up the westerlies to the Cape of Good Hope. In these voyages, as indeed in any made under sail, the importance of ocean currents and, when coasting, of tides cannot be overemphasised. One need only observe that this same route to the Cape was followed by merchant sail for as long as the latter lasted, and for the same reasons, even though the great steel barques of the early 20th century were infinitely superior in sailing qualities to their predecessors of some 400 years earlier.

The carrack increased in size in the early years of the 16th century and is typified in the painting *c* 1520 of Portuguese carracks (see p.19) tentatively attributed to the school of Patenir. The vessels shown have all the characteristics of the earlier carracks, in particular the ratio of 3:2:1 in length on deck, length of keel and beam. However, these proportions, to which all the maritime nations seem to have adhered fairly strictly until about 1530, exaggerated the lack of weatherliness in the ships. The innovations in rigging shown in the painting are minor and, although they may have contributed more power, did little to improve the sailing qualities to windward. The most obvious developments occurred at the turn of the century, and were the introduction of the main topgallant sail, and the fore topsail and the fitting of a fourth mast, the bonaventure mizzen.

Both these latter features were made possible by the lengthening of the ships as they became larger. In the first, the greater length enabled the foremast to be brought just sufficiently aft for it to be stepped on the keel. As a consequence, the mast could be heavier and not only take the weight of a topsail but also that of a fore course made larger. Nor did this arrangement negate the original purpose of the foresail, which was to assist in controlling the ship's head. That was now the prime function of the spritsail.

The additional lateen mizzen sail was of necessity relatively small, for the bonaventure mizzen mast was stepped right aft near the taffrail with the heel probably on one of the main deck beams. We do not know for certain the reason for introducing this sail although it certainly appeared at much the same time as the fore topsail. Perhaps it was designed to counter the additional leverage at the bow caused by the greater sail area on the fore mast; it seems to have been too small to have any real effect in the performance to windward of so cumbersome a vessel.

Portuguese carracks, *c* 1520. Unknown artist after the school of Patenir. The carracks in this painting were carefully drawn by an artist who understood what he saw, which makes it a valuable piece of documentary evidence. The heavy construction and broad beam is shown together with the huge fore and aftercastles, the cause of so much windage that Hawkins and others sought later to reduce.

However, this was not of vital importance to the two nations concerned at that time with trans-oceanic trade, Spain and Portugal. After all, routes had been discovered to and from the Indies and the Americas which could perfectly safely be used by the existing square-rigged great ships whether we call them *naos* or carracks. There was no real incentive to improve their performance, as there was no possible way in which they could have been improved to the extent that would really have been worthwhile, by enabling them to make an additional voyage in a season. Although Spain and Portugal regarded each other with some suspicion they were not rivals in the Indies, and the Pope had arbitrarily divided the New World between them in 1493, an arrangement adjusted between the two countries by the Treaty of Tordisellas the following year.

The first real steps to improve the sailing qualities of great ships seem to have followed upon developments in the use of the ship as a weapon of war. With the exception in some cases of the Mediterranean galley, in which the low beakhead was used as a ram, the traditional method of fighting at sea had for centuries been simply the use of ships as floating platforms from which soldiers could fight in the contemporary manner of the period. It was essentially hand-to-hand combat with spears and swords, preceded generally by the use of lime-pots, and volleys of stones, arrows and spears or anything else that could usefully be used as a projectile. To this end, with the tactical commonsense that a man fighting from a higher level has an advantage, the tops and castles had been developed. Little had changed at first, following the introduction of gunpowder and the use of small guns, which at best could only be described as man-killers. Very early in the 16th century, however, much larger guns were introduced, guns sufficiently large that their weight in the castles or even on the deck posed a threat to the vessel's stability. They had therefore to be taken as far down into the ship as possible and fired through a specially cut hole in the ship's side: a gun-port. Although the gun-port had a hinged lid which could be closed when the gun-port was not in use, it had of necessity to be cut well above the water-line – a statement of the obvious justified by the number of ships which, during the following hundred years or so, either foundered or else were ineffective because their gun-ports were too low to be used other than in calm weather.

By the 1520s the use of gun ports on a battery deck had become firmly established although the heavy gun still was probably not considered as the principal armament. The *Henry Grâce à Dieu* of 1514, flagship of Henry VIII, is listed as carrying 184 guns but probably fewer than twenty were much more than man-killers. Tradition has it that the *Mary Rose* of 1509, sunk in 1545 – and currently the subject of investigation that, it is hoped, will lead to her recovery – was the first English ship to have gun ports below the upper deck.

At about this time the shape of the ships began to change, as far as one may judge from the rather imprecise illustrations of the day. The reasons are not clear although as it occurred at roughly the same time as the widespread adoption of heavier guns there is a considerable and reasonable temptation to link the two. The evidence suggests that shortly after the introduction of heavy guns (for their day) aboard ships there was seen to be a need for being able to manoeuvre the ships more adroitly, the better to use the new weapon. Perhaps 16th century seamen quickly appreciated the great advantage of being able to cross the enemy's bow or stern and rake the length of the decks through the relatively weaker construction and lighter defence at these points. If so, the manoeuvring for position to cripple the enemy before boarding becomes important enough to demand an improvement in the ship's performance. Unfortunately, although there is nothing which negates this conclusion, there is little positive evidence to support it. However, if this is not the case it is difficult to see why improved sailing qualities should be more important for fighting with guns than when manoeuvring for a favourable position from which to close and board.

The alternative is to assume that the change towards more weatherly proportions from the late 1520s was purely coincidental, but if this is so, why not earlier? The importance of a ship's proportions in relation to her sailing ability had long been appreciated – *vide* the caravel – but the 3:2:1 ratio had been preferred because of the cargo carrying capacity it provided. For more than half a century this 'round' hull had been preferred and it seems reasonable to assume that it would have continued so until another factor forced itself into consideration: the need for improved handling qualities brought about by the advent at sea of the heavy gun. In England at least,

the introduction of the gun battery below the upper deck was followed by a major change in construction. Until the early years of the 16th century English ships were planked in the edge-joined clinker fashion but this method of building proved inadequate for the stresses and strains to which the hull was now subjected, not only by the firing of the guns but also probably by the concentration of weight thrust in differing directions as the ship moved to the motion of the sea. Further, with the structure already strained to the utmost there was no possibility of lengthening it as the need for more mobility demanded. As a consequence warships in England – and most other Northern European countries that had clung to the clinker tradition – turned wholeheartedly to the form of construction using the non edge-joined flush planking commonly but erroneously, for the term means many things, called carvel building.

There is evidence that at first some ships were built in a mixture of the two traditions but by the 1540s clinker-building was no longer considered for

Jesus of Lübeck. This is the only known representation of the *Jesus of Lübeck*. The hull is probably accurately drawn but it is doubtful whether this rig was actually used as lateen mizzen topsails were most impractical. There is no contemporary illustration of such sails in use.

warships of any consequence. In merchant vessels too the practice died out except in the case of some of the smaller types. For these in some areas the tradition was continued until even as late as the end of the 19th century. Depictions of great ships from the later 1520s onwards suggest that the proportions of 3:2:1 were losing favour with the result that hulls were relatively narrower and had lost the 'round' look of the Portuguese carracks. Typical of this new proportion were the carracks *Henry Grâce à Dieu* of 1514, known as the *Great Harry*, and the *Jesus of Lübeck* (see p.21). The former was built as a warship, the latter might properly be described as a well-armed merchant ship. Bought for the navy in 1544 she was frequently leased to merchants by the Crown. The *Jesus* was lost to the Spaniards at San Juan de Uloa in 1568 and in the process had a considerable if indirect influence on ship design in the crucial years of the reign of Elizabeth.

This trend towards improving the design of the big ships of the day produced the most widely known of all the sailing ships, the galleon. The origin of the name is obscure. Its sound suggests an affinity with, even a development from, the much older 'galley', but this is belied by its appearance. The origin of the name is obscured by the apparently indiscriminate use by all the maritime nations of the word 'galley' and its many derivatives. The term 'galleon' may have come from 'galley' through the oared sailing vessel known as a galleass, which will be considered later, but the evidence is confused and conflicting.

As with the three-masted ship, there is no clear evidence as to which country first developed the galleon, but it seems most likely to have come from Spain. Good sailing qualities were the prerequisite for a defensible ship, for almost by definition the first requirement was for a 'nimble' ship as the 17th century expression had it, to enable her gunners to make the best use of their ordnance. In the second

quarter of the 16th century, when the galleon appeared, the country with most need for defensible ships was Spain. The vessels of Portugal, it is true, carried most valuable cargoes from the Indies but most of their cargo was in goods. The Spanish *flota* on the other hand carried more immediately tangible wealth in the form of gold and silver. Furthermore the appearance of French ships in the waters of the Caribbean during the wars between France and Spain between 1521 and 1559 posed a direct threat to Spanish shipping. From 1522 onwards the Spanish ships sailing to the New World had to be much more heavily armed than had previously been necessary when rebellious ill-armed Indians had constituted the only opposition. By 1526 French successes had led to the order that Spanish vessels had to sail in company and be covered by warships in the areas where they were bound to make a landfall (the islands of the Azores and the Canaries, and Cape St Vincent). All these measures proved ineffective and in 1543 the passage of Spanish ships to and from the Americas was regulated in the form of annual convoys – the *flota*. Spain, therefore, had every reason to seek ways of improving the sailing qualities of her ships in order to provide the best defence for the treasure fleet. However, although the place of origin of the galleon is of interest academically it is of little significance in practice. As we have seen earlier, the very nature of the seaman's trade made it virtually impossible to keep secret for long any major changes in design or construction of ships. Within a very few years galleons were in the service of Spain, Portugal, Genoa, Venice and England.

The rig of the galleon was very similar to that which had been established for the carrack: spritsail, course and topsail on the foremast; course, topsail and topgallant on the main; lateen and lateen topsail on the mizzen and a lateen sail on the bonaventure mast.

The main difference lay in the shape of the hull and in particular, the bow. The proportions of the hull were narrower than those of the earlier carracks but little different from those of the later carracks, with a keel to beam ratio of 2.3 : 1. This elongation of the hull was an undoubted step towards improving sailing to windward and it was materially assisted by the redesigned upperworks in the bow. In the carrack (see p.21) the forecastle was built out forward of the stem. This arrangement may have had some advantage in fighting, although it is difficult to see what, but it had distinct disadvantages in terms of sailing. The effect of weight so far forward was to press the ship's head lower into the water, making her more sluggish. In addition, the windage created by the superstructure so far forward exerted a considerable leverage on the bow. At times this could be useful, but unlike the spritsail, so placed to exact the same effect, the leverage caused by the upperworks could not be controlled because they were a permanent feature.

In the galleon, both these disadvantages of weight and windage were reduced by withdrawing the superstructure of the forecastle almost entirely within the body of the ship; *i.e.* it was set abaft the stem rather than forward of it (see p.26). It will readily be seen that the removal of weight so far forward would tend to lift the bow, so easing the vessel's passage through the water. Similarly, by moving the forecastle slightly aft, and so reducing the leverage caused by having the superstructure so far forward, the ship's head would be easier to control. The most obvious characteristic of the galleon was the long beakhead which projected forward from the stem, instead of the trapezoidal platform that had supported the forward part of the carrack forecastle.

The Fall of Icarus, Pieter Brueghel, 1530?-1569. The ship depicted is a carrack, *c* 1550. Described as 'high-charged', these vessels were difficult to sail well because of the windage caused by the high forecastle and poop, often called the summercastle.

This type of ship dominated the long distance trade routes until the end of the 16th century and as a warship it was supreme until 1588 when it was eclipsed by another form of galleon developed in England, largely as a result of the action between Spanish ships and John Hawkins's men in the *Jesus of Lübeck* at San Juan de Uloa in 1568. Once again, the disposition of heavy ordnance aboard warships and the manner of its tactical employment played a vital role in changing their design.

Neither the politics which led to the action nor the details of the fight concern us here, except in one particular – the tactics employed on that occasion by Hawkins. Trapped in harbour and outnumbered in both ships and men, Hawkins had hauled the *Jesus* and the *Minion* clear of the enemy who was intent upon boarding. Then, standing off, although at very short range, he engaged the three Spanish vessels with his heavy battery guns only. Unable to manoeuvre and close with the English ships, one Spanish vessel was destroyed by an explosion, presumably in the magazine, whilst the other two were so battered that they sank in the shallow waters of the bay. The *Jesus*, already old, leaking and a poor sailer, had to be abandoned, but the *Minion* provided a means of escape.

The lessons of the battle were not lost upon the Navy Board, which was responsible for the administration of England's navy. Two men dominated the administration during the crucial years before 1588, in the positions of Surveyor, responsible for the design, building and upkeep of the Queen's ships, and the Treasurer who, having managed to obtain money for the navy from the strictly controlled royal purse, then had to see that it was spent to the best effect. Sir William Wynter was Surveyor of the Navy from 1557 until 1589, as well as Master of the Ordnance of the Navy. The Treasurer, from 1578 until his death in 1595 was Hawkins himself. Whatever personal rivalries divided them, Wynter and Hawkins

An English warship, *c* 1580. This little drawing appears in *Fragments of Ancient Shipwrightry* (see p.25) and may be intended to represent one of the Elizabethan galleons before the new designs introduced in 1581. It has no beakhead, a feature of the Hawkins ships, but the forecastle is drawn back inboard aft of the stem. The rig is interesting in that there are only three masts. The sail plan is simple with no topgallants at all and no mizzen lateen topsail; the sails in accordance with those of the new ships planned are cut to set much 'flatter'.

were at one both in their determination to provide Queen Elizabeth with the best warships in the world and in the methods by which it should be done.

In 1569, the year following San Juan de Uloa, the scale of ordnance with which the Queen's ships were equipped was reduced drastically. The *Henry Grâce à Dieu (Great Harry)* of 1545 is recorded as having carried 251 guns. By contrast, in accordance with the scale of 1569, one of the largest of Queen Elizabeth's warships, the *Triumph* (1561), carried only 68 guns and of these 26 were mankillers. The *Triumph* was one of the four major warships in service in 1588 that pre-dated the appointment of Hawkins to the Navy Board, and might therefore be termed 'Spanish galleon' in type and an improvement on the carrack as a warship. There is little detailed evidence of the weight of ordnance and its precise disposition at this date. However, we know that the *Great Elizabeth* of 1514 carried a total of 120 guns in her castles, of which 84 were serpentines weighing about 250 lbs each–suggesting a total weight in guns alone of nearly 15 tons, above the main deck. She also carried six serpentines and a stone gun (perier) in the main and mizzen tops.

This reappraisal of the use of ordnance, however, had to be considered alongside the other lesson learned by Hawkins, that to be effective in their new role the guns themselves must be protected against boarding. This could be achieved most effectively by fitting them into ships that could outsail the enemy, and so dictate the way in which the battle was fought. The result was the English galleon, the sailing qualities of which so surprised the Duke of Medina-Sidonia and his officers of the Spanish Armada.

The most readily apparent changes made in the design of English ships were the reduction of the fore and aftercastles. This was a logical extension of the earlier development of withdrawing the forecastle within the compass of the hull and was carried out to achieve the same purpose: a reduction of the windage which so hampered sailing to windward. This is evident in the contemporary illustrations reproduced on p.26 when compared with Brueghel's mid-century galleons on p.23. The reduction of the upperworks was accompanied by an improvement in stability, not only because of the reduced castles but also because the new armament both reduced weight in absolute terms and placed low in the ship a greater proportion of what remained. It may be that Hawkins was influenced in this reduction of the upperworks by the galleass, a warship for both rowing and sailing and which was certainly low in profile.

Drastic changes were also made in the cut of the sails. It had been the fashion in the 15th and early 16th centuries to cut square sails generously, presumably on the theory that the greater the area on which the wind can act, the greater the power and therefore the faster the ship will travel. However, whilst this theory has some validity when the wind is well aft and the ship is running, sails that are too amply cut will not set well if the wind is forward of the quarter, and they are much less efficient to windward. Because the essential requirement for the new ships was that they should be nimble, Hawkins had the sails cut much flatter.

The result of both these changes in design are well illustrated in *Fragments of Ancient Shipwrightry*, manuscripts almost certainly the work of Matthew Baker (1530-1613), the leading shipwright of the last 30 years of the reign of Elizabeth. Baker was closely concerned in the rebuilding of the navy under the direction of Hawkins, and the drawings supply an important clue to another possible change in design.

The improvements already discussed would undoubtedly have had a marked effect on the performance of the ships concerned. However, the difference in the sailing qualities of the English and Spanish warships was so great that one suspects that there

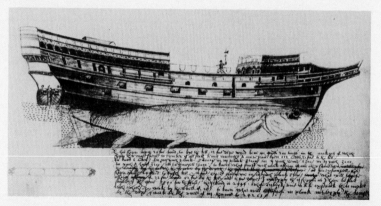

(below) An English galleon, c 1586. This Matthew Baker drawing of a sail plan for a ship of 300 tons to carry 30–32 guns shows no topsails on the two mizzen masts. Lateen topsails such as shown in the *Anthony Rolls* (1545) would have been extremely cumbersome to use. Notice the long beakhead, designed to keep the low forecastle as dry as possible in a heavy sea.

(above) Underwater lines c 1586. This drawing, from *Fragments of Ancient Shipwrightry* by Matthew Baker (see p.25), was evidently to demonstrate to a layman the ideal shape for the hull below the waterline. It shows one of the smaller English galleons. The dimensions: keel 60 ft, beam 24 ft, depth of hold 12 ft and tonnage 200, most nearly approximate to those of the *Crane* (1590) in the list of Elizabethan warships: keel 60 ft, beam 26 ft, depth of hold 13 ft, tonnage 202, 19 guns.

(below) Draught of an English galleon, c 1586. A draught from *Fragments of Ancient Shipwrightry* showing the section through the hull at four positions.

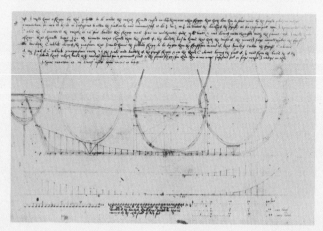

may also have been a considerable improvement in the underwater shape of the hull. The evidence is slight and circumstantial, but it may explain the superiority in sailing of English ships.

There are three drawings in *Fragments of Ancient Shipwrightry* which show the same underwater hull in profile although the upperworks differ slightly (see p.26). The first has a sail plan; in the second the hull outline has the shape in section superimposed at four different positions; in the third a drawing of a fish is superimposed on the hull below the waterline. The key seems to lie in the third drawing, which it is clear was deliberately drawn not quite as a profile, so that the after end of the forecastle and the stern can be seen. In this drawing there is a hatched area to represent water, down through which below the stern a vertical line continues, to meet the line of the keel at right angles suggesting another hull form with a deeper stern section and a clumsy run aft.

The hatched area is so squared at the ends that it is inconceivable that it was meant to portray with any real accuracy the hull shape of other ships of the time. Nevertheless, the shading at the stern is clearly intended to convey a message, so one may guess that the shaded area is meant to give a general impression of the disadvantages of certain hull forms, and so enhance the advantages of the new proposal. Taken as an exaggerated view then, and compared with the depictions of carracks of the period, the use of the hatched drawing to make a particular and important point becomes understandable.

A contemporary drawing of a Spanish ship suggests that by 1588 at least, and no doubt in the galleons developed in mid-century, the underwater lines of Spanish vessels were much better than those suggested by the shading on Baker's drawing (see p.26). However this may be, one cannot ignore the evidence of the eye-witnesses on both sides in the Armada fight as to the vast superiority in the sailing qualities of the English ships.

In the 'fish drawing', if we may so call it, Baker seems to be showing a hull form that is a considerable advance on another presumably more common shape in use at that time. The sections shown in the second drawing conform roughly to what one might expect the 'fish-hull' drawing to represent at those positions, and, significantly, the line showing the rise of floor conforms almost exactly to the line described by the underside of the fish.

As we have produced the fish drawing as evidence of some weight in indicating what may have been a major change in hull design, perhaps we should consider why it should have been made. The idea that it represents mere decoration can be dismissed immediately. Neither its position on the drawing, nor the manner of its depiction, nor in fact the style of the drawing suggests that the fish is meant as the sort of fanciful embellishment often to be found on charts of the period. It seems reasonable then to accept the fish drawing as demonstrating something new, otherwise one can see little reason for its presence.

It is possible that the drawing was part of Matthew Baker's thought process in working out the shape he wanted for the underwater body. This seems unlikely however, for one would expect such a drawing to be less finished – much more of a sketch. The alternative is that it was meant to convey Baker's ideas to someone else; but presumably not another shipwright, for a simple sketch of the sections would have sufficed for that. The likeliest explanation must surely be that so finished a drawing was for someone, or some persons, of consequence. Persons, furthermore, who would not readily understand even the simple technical drawings which the shipbuilder commonly used. The purpose of the fish was to convey the unusual body shape to the viewer. There is little or no shading on the drawing to suggest curves or contours, but everyone would be familiar with the shape of a fish. Consciously or unconsciously chosen, the concept was a brilliant one, for not only did it give a good idea of the body shape intended, but it also demonstrated far more effectively than any words that the purpose of the new shape was to allow the vessel to slip through the water as easily as possible. In this last regard the drawing was even more effective than a model, which would certainly have been used for the purpose a hundred years later, and may even have been used in Baker's day.

But for whom was the drawing intended? Perhaps the Navy Board, although it seems unlikely that the two key figures, Wynter and Hawkins would have needed quite so graphic a presentation. It seems more likely that the drawing was produced for someone of even grander station. In 1579 Hawkins obtained permission to finance the building of 25 vessels of all types, the immediate responsibility for their design and construction being placed in the hands of Joseph Pett and Matthew Baker, two of the three Master Shipwrights to the Queen. In view of the parsimonious manner in which Elizabethan finances were handled it is more than probable that Hawkins had to convince Lord Burghley, Lord High Treasurer and the Queen's chief minister – and probably Queen Elizabeth herself – that the money would be well spent. Burghley and the Queen were exactly the sort of people for whom Baker's fish-drawing would have the most meaning.

The English galleon brought no startling change in rig, except perhaps in the cut of the sails already noted. We have mentioned too, the introduction early in the century of the fourth mast, the bona-venture mizzen, and it has been suggested by historians that four masts were fitted in all major vessels, particularly warships, for the remainder of the 16th century and well into the next. Undoubtedly the four-masted rig was commonly in use until at least the mid-1620s, but there is in Fragments of Ancient Shipwrightry a drawing of one of the Queen's ships which has the three-masted rig. This, from so reputable a source, together with the several paintings of Dutch ships with three masts very early in the 17th century suggests that the four-masted rig was not quite so completely adopted for the ships of northern and western Europe as has sometimes been supposed.

With three masts, the rig comprised a spritsail, course and topsail on the foremast, course, topsail and topgallant sails on the main mast and a lateen mizzen sail. With the four-masted rig a lateen-topsail may sometimes have been rigged on the mizzen (third) mast. However, this sail would have been difficult to handle and it is significantly absent from any of the Matthew Baker drawings.

For the English galleon then, there is considerable documentary evidence that crucial changes were made in the size and shape of the upperworks. There is some evidence, almost entirely circumstantial and rather more open to dispute, that sails were cut differently and that an improved underwater hull form was introduced. What cannot be disputed however is the performance of the ships themselves when the day came against which they had been conceived and built. The difference between the English galleons and those of the enemy was never better displayed than on their first encounter, on 21 July 1588. Warned of the Armada's approach, Earl Howard of Effingham, Lord High Admiral, had warped his ships out of Plymouth on the night of 19–20 July. The next evening Spanish look-outs saw their topsails in the late sunlight ahead and to leeward. Soon after dawn with a brisk wind from the west-north-west, Medina–Sidonia's fleet of 130 ships of all types, including some 30 fighting galleons was sailing easily a little under ten miles west of the Eddystone rocks. The wind was some 20° or so abaft the beam to port, and the Spanish commander was comfortable in the knowledge that his ships were on almost their best point of sailing, and that he had the windward position. Inshore, a number of English ships were beating westward, presumably hoping to come up behind the Armada after it had passed. It was then that the Spanish commanders, who had a respect for English seamanship that was mutual, received a surprise and learned for the first time just how weatherly the new English warships were, for the main English fleet came suddenly into view behind them *i.e.* to windward. And while they were still pondering on the weatherliness of ships that could apparently work round to windward of them with ease, they saw the squadron already noticed on the landward side change course and, crossing ahead of the great Armada then tack to join Howard and the main body of the English fleet to windward.

The Spaniards had thought their ships (the galleons) swift and capable of going well to windward but this was apparently not the only way in which the English ships demonstrated their superiority. An eye-witness wrote, 'The speediest vessels in the Armada . . . seemed in comparison to be standing still.'

We are not concerned here with the story of the Armada fight of 1588 nor even to what extent the Hawkins-Wynter plan to fight by cannonade alone succeeded or failed. The question of ordnance is relevant to our subject only insofar as it had a profound effect on ship design – a design that was successful in enabling the English commanders to dictate the conduct of the series of engagements that made up the great 'battle'. Suffice to say that, thereafter, all major western warships were derivations of the galleon type until the mid-19th century.

So far we have been concerned with the major developments of ship design in the 16th century, all of which can be shown in the external view of the hull. There were other improvements and innovations internally, which although not major factors in the mainstream of development as discussed so far,

were nevertheless significant in their contribution to the strength of the vessel and its seaworthiness. Before discussing these improvements it may be of value to dwell briefly on the basic method of construction and the general layout of these vessels.

The method of construction was that which remained standard until the mid-19th century. The keel was laid and fastened to the stempost at the bow and the sternpost at the stern and to the strengthening keelson immediately above. To this backbone were fastened the frames which conformed to the desired shape of the hull (see p.26). The frames were locked together by the transverse beams which supported the deck, and which ran from the frames on one side to those opposite on the other; by the planking outside and by the ceiling (also planked) on the inside of the frames, and by great timbers called wales which girdled the ship fore and aft round the frames. The timbers were fastened with treenails (pegs) made of oak and wrought iron bolts which were driven through holes drilled in the timber and then clenched (bent over, usually through a washer) on the other side. Oak was the most favoured timber.

Below the upper deck there was one gun deck, usually but not invariably, continuous from stem to stern. Sometimes from roughly below the beginning of the quarterdeck, the gun deck was stepped down for the remainder of its length aft. This enabled the deck above also to be stepped, permitting either a further reduction in height of the upperworks aft or more probably higher deckheads and greater comfort in the officers' cabins, which were situated above on the quarterdeck and poop. Below the gun deck ran an orlop deck from the bows to the galley, or cookeroom as it was called, amidships. On the orlop deck were cabins for the petty officers: the boatswain, gunner, carpenter and perhaps the surgeon if one were carried. The men were quartered on the main or gun deck.

One innovation of the period was the use of pillars to provide additional support to deck beams. They could only be placed above other deck beams, of course, or in the case of those under the orlop or the stepped gun deck aft, on the keel. Riders, heavy transverse frames fitted internally above the ceiling, seem also to have been introduced at about this time for they were added to the *White Bear* (1564) in the 1580s, twenty years after she was built. The introduction of the chain pump at this time was also credited to Hawkins. These innovations are shown here as being introduced to English ships, but there is so little evidence that one cannot be sure that they were actually first used on board English vessels. However, as it is apparent that the English shipwrights were among the most progressive in Europe and their galleons the most technologically advanced, it seems reasonable to suppose that even if the ideas noted immediately above were not actually English in origin they were very soon adopted by Baker, Pett and their colleagues, so that this is at least a fairly close indication of the time that they were first used effectively. A case in point is the introduction of separate topmasts that could be struck, 'a wonderful ease to great ships', as Sir Walter Raleigh put it. They are first mentioned at about this time and Hawkins has also been credited with their invention. It may be, however, that he merely introduced them to the Queen's ships and that the striking topmast was actually first produced in about 1570 by a seaman from Enkhuizen, a village north of Amsterdam, as has also been claimed.

One other type of 16th century warship should be noted, if only to explain why it was not adopted by the northern seafaring nations, the most prominent of which were now England and Holland. Large vessels, either warships or merchant vessels that could be either rowed or sailed, were referred to by almost all the maritime nations quite indiscriminately as galleys, galleasses or simply oared galleons. It will be convenient here to use the term 'galleass', although the distinction between galley and galleass as referring to oared vessels and oared sailing vessels respectively is false and seems to have arisen in the 19th century.

The square-rigged oared vessel which came to be known as the galleass was introduced at the beginning of the 16th century in an attempt to bring to the northern waters, or at least those west of the Straits of Gibraltar, the freedom of movement that galleys (most of them lateen assisted) had enjoyed in the relatively calmer waters of the Mediterranean Sea. The temptation to have ships free of the constraints of the wind is understandable and if the galleass was persevered with by Spain and Venice longer than by the Northern Powers it must also be said that the latter also flirted with the idea for many years. The *Kateryn* of 1512 had thirty oars and three masts with topsails on the fore and the main, and there were at least two other similar vessels. In a list of 1546 there are a number of vessels called galleasses but whether they could in fact be rowed is uncertain. The illustration of one of them in the Anthony Roll in the Pepysian Library of Magdalene College, Cambridge suggests not. There were certainly royal ships listed as galleys throughout the reign of the Tudors, but they seem to have been little used and in mid-century (1551 and 1554) official reports from London to Venice contain the uncompromising words 'They do not use galleys'. To a Venetian, a galley was essentially a vessel easily propelled by oars. The last recorded occasions of these vessels being used were in 1563 and 1586. Nevertheless, the notion still lingered that they might be useful vessels, presumably in defence of the Thames estuary, for in 1601 and 1602 four new galleys were built. They remained a charge to the Crown until 1629 but there is no record of any one of them having seen service at sea.

Spain was probably the greatest protagonist of the galleass, four of which formed part of Medina-Sidonia's fighting squadrons in 1588. They were manoeuvrable and powerfully-armed vessels but they were not suitable for northern waters. They were low in the water and of relatively light construction, both of which could prove their undoing in heavy seas. In this instance, however, it was not that the weather nullified their advantage by threatening to swamp them or cause them to founder. Rather their advantage was discounted because there were so rarely conditions of near calm, when they were unable to use their greatest asset to the best purpose. This, rather than their light construction, is probably the reason why the galleass was never a powerful force in the northern fleets.

We have traced the main course of the development of the ship in the 16th century through the warship. But although this was perhaps the most important facet of its evolution, other quite significant steps were being taken in the design of merchant vessels, which were to have far-reaching effects in the next century. Whilst the English authorities were concentrating on producing the best warships in the world, the Dutch went on quietly developing merchant vessels for special purposes until, by the end of the 16th century, they had the most efficient carriers afloat. They then had to set about protecting them as trade and prosperity grew, and in particular protecting them from the English who, having established themselves as the dominant sea-power of the northern world, sought for means by which to profit from their new situation. The next chapter offers a brief survey of the merchant ships of England and Holland in the 16th century, about which, alas, all too little is known.

The *Golden Lion*, 1582, Visscher. The *Golden Lion* was one of the earliest of the newly designed English galleons and is depicted with topgallant sails on the fore and main and with a lateen mizzen topsail. 'Crows feet', seen at the upper ends of the lateen yards, were fashionable in rigging from about 1575-1650 in the belief that they eased strain by spreading the load. The untidy-looking loops hanging from the furled courses are the martnets, which, led forward, were used to keep the luff (or leading edge) of the sail taught.

On the left of the picture is a rare illustration of a galleass (but commonly called a galley by Elizabethans) in the English service.

Dutch and English Shipping to 1600

The ships of the 15th and 16th centuries are unfortunately, in all but a very few cases, merely names—names of individual vessels and names of types. In many cases we know their relative sizes because their tonnage is listed, but only very rarely do we have dimensions to represent an absolute size which has any meaning. We know the ports used but we often cannot tell the port of sailing for incoming ships or the destination of outgoing vessels. Worst and most frustrating of all, we rarely know what they looked like, still less how they were constructed. Very occasionally we are able to see in a 16th century illustration recognisable types of the 17th century. Rather more often we are tempted to give 17th century characteristics to a 16th or even 15th century vessel merely because of the similarity of the name. The hazards of this particular exercise are demonstrated by the history of the *boier*. This was originally a two-masted vessel which dropped out of use towards the end of the 17th century, but by the middle of the 18th century the name was firmly established as denoting a round-sterned craft used for pleasure sailing. In the 20th century the term destroyer has meant a number of different sizes of warship fulfilling at least three different roles over a similar 60 year period. The pitfalls in the way of the historian who assumes that because a name implied a particular rig and or hull form in 1600, the same name denoted similar characteristics in 1400 or at any time in between, are numerous.

As the tonnage figures quoted will be significant in relating the size of various types of ship, we should consider what the term means and how the name

arose. Different units of measurement were used by the various maritime nations of Europe to measure the carrying capacity of a ship's hull. The Scandinavian countries used the *last*, equivalent to approximately 4000 lbs weight, Venice the *botta* and both England and France the tun, the capacity of a Bordeaux wine cask—indicative of the extent of that trade between the two countries. The tun held approximately 252 gallons, but because of the awkward shape of the cask itself and the ship's hull into which it had to be stowed it is not surprising that a tun, as a measure of a ship's carrying capacity, should eventually reflect the wasted space and be taken to occupy 40 cubic feet instead of 33 cubic feet. Moreover, as the tun became accepted as the standard unit it also was equated with a fixed weight of 2240 lbs to represent the equivalent weight of other goods. Tons (burden) roughly approximated to modern net tonnage, tons and tonnage to the modern gross tonnage. However, the method used to calculate either figure was the subject of considerable and constant dispute. Figures recorded therefore can be safely used only as a guide to relative size between ships of any one period.

One of the first English vessels we should note is the balinger. In the 15th century the records show these vessels to be commonly of between 25 and 60 tons and occasionally as large as 120 tons. In the early part of the century oars are mentioned, and the size of the crew, 22 men or more for a vessel of 40 tons, seems to confirm that the oars were an important feature of the rig. There is no hard evidence as to why this was the case although there may be a clue in the accounts of William Catton, clerk of the ships in the time of Henry V (1413-1422). The *George de la Toure* was fitted with two masts, each of which carried one sail. A reference to bonnets for each sail suggests that at this date both were square sails. If this were so one could see that a full complement of oarsmen would be required to enable the ship to make a passage to Bordeaux or some other Biscayan port in the teeth of the prevailing south-westerly winds. On the return voyage she would be sailing easily most of the time making good use of her square sails. It may be significant in this regard that according to Dorothy Burwash, *English Merchant Shipping 1460-1540*, p.107, the records show that by far the greatest number of English balingers seem to have traded out of ports in Devon and Cornwall, which would have given them the shortest passage to the Biscayan coast under oars.

The balinger had ceased to become a seagoing vessel of any significance by the reign of Elizabeth (1558-1603) perhaps because the introduction of the lateen mizzen to Northern Europe had enabled ships to make the outward passage more regularly under sail. The name 'balinger' is of some interest although its origins are obscure. It almost certainly derives from *baleine* (Fr.), meaning whale. Two conflicting theories have been put forward, the first that it is merely a corruption of 'baleiner', *i.e.* a boat used for whaling; the second that it stems also from the hull shape – high in the bows and low aft, similar to the silhouette of a whale. Whatever the origins of the name, the connection with whaling is reinforced by the fact that balingers were most common in, although by no means exclusive to, the waters adjacent to the Bay of Biscay, one of the earliest European whale fisheries.

In English records of the 14th century almost all the larger carriers are referred to as cogs or, particularly if they originated from the Biscayan coast or further south, cocks – an Anglicised version of the French *coques* or perhaps the Italian *cocca*. As they are contemporaneous we must assume that all these references are indeed to ships of the type described earlier and typified by the Bremen cog illustrated on p.7.

As the cog was replaced first by the hulc and then by the carrack, the sea-going version disappeared, though numerous members of the family of the cog survived in use on sheltered waters into the present century. By the mid-15th century the reference to an English cog was a comparative rarity in the records and foreign cogs were almost invariably from Holland and of 10-50 tons burden. Somewhat similar in size was the crayer, a small sailing vessel usually of between 25 and 50 tons. We cannot be certain about the rig for the previous century, although there is evidence that in the first half of the 16th century just before their decline in use, crayers might have had two or three masts and their rig included a main topsail. Despite the name, crayers seem but rarely to have been used as fishing vessels; they were largely used in the cross-channel trade.

Two other types of small craft which disappear in the 16th century after two centuries or more in common use are picards and farcosts. The former, which are first recorded in the 1320s, were – at least in Henry VIII's time – single-masted vessels of between 12 and 40 tons. From the beginning the records suggest that they were not often used as traders in the normal sense but rather as simple carriers. They were frequently used to take out salt and victuals to the fishing fleets, returning laden with the latter's catch, a practice which greatly increased the effectiveness and profitability of the fishermen. Picards were rarely used as fishing vessels themselves however. Another common and widespread employment for them was as lighters, loading or unloading ships that could not – or more probably perhaps for various reasons would not – find a berth.

It must be remembered that a port is still a legally defined area which includes not only the harbour but also all its beaches and creeks, and this is because until the late 19th century by far the great proportion of cargoes were loaded and discharged over open beaches in between tides. Where there were quays,

Dogger, c 1665, Willem van de Velde (the Younger). Fishing boats known as doggers preceded the buss in the North Sea fishery in the 14th century, but little is known of their hull form or rig. It is reasonable to suppose that they were not unlike the buss in shape, because of their employment, and this drawing of a 17th century dogger shows a similarity. However, whether this is derived from the original dogger or whether the hull was gradually changed to a form that had proved itself in the buss is not clear.

loading or unloading was faster only because it was easier from a wharf than from a beach. The ship still had to spend much the same time because it dried out alongside the quay.

Unlike some types of craft, notably the balinger as we have seen, the picard was not apparently favoured in one region rather than another. Records show them to have used ports from the east coast of Scotland all the way round to the River Severn, and in Ireland.

The enigma of the types of vessel in use during the period covered by this brief survey is the farcost. Although there are frequent references to them, particularly in the mid-15th century, we know very little

about them and nothing of their rig. This might lead one to suppose that the name may have been a general term used of small vessels large enough to trade across the North Sea or the English Channel, *i.e.* a 'farcoast', but this as a general term is belied by the only type of vessel whose name arose under similar circumstances. The bilander, Dutch in origin and a coaster meant to sail 'by the land', was a particular type of vessel recognisable by its rig. The farcost and the picard both disappear from the records in the 16th century.

Contemporary with the picard was the spinace, of which it would seem the 16th and 17th century term 'pinnace' is a corruption. The spinace was a decked vessel, frequently oared as well as rigged for sailing, and was often used as a tender to the great warships. From 10 to 50 tons in size, spinaces traded across the Channel and as far south as Spain.

The caravel was introduced to English waters in the middle of the 15th century, probably in its square-rigged form. The accounts of Sir John Howard (1430?-1485), later, as Duke of Norfolk, the Lord Admiral (1483-1485), show that he had a caravel built in 1463. Most interesting however is the mention of a spritsail. Portugal alone among the maritime nations of the Atlantic retained the predominantly lateen rig (*i.e.* square-rigged on the fore, lateen rigged on the other masts) for the caravel until the end of the 16th century (Martinez-Hidalgo). This suggests that for the other countries the caravel may already have been losing its identity and becoming merely another version of the square-rigged ship. If this is so, it is more easily understood how 50–60 years later when the name might almost have lost any significance as denoting a particular type of vessel, that name, or a corruption of it (carvel), could be transferred to meaning a singular method of planking which was first introduced to England by that type of vessel. It is interesting that once more the largest

recorded English caravel was of some 50 tons and that like several other types of ship mentioned earlier, the name dropped out of use in the 16th century. Clearly, so successful a ship did not actually fall into disuse; only the original name was lost as the form of hull was adopted and perhaps adapted as the standard for vessels of a similar size. For example, one such type of vessel might well have been the pinnace as it was called, roughly from this same time onwards. The deep-sea pinnace of 30 plus tons was of a size with the caravel, worked the same sort of voyages and trades and already had a three-masted rig. There is no real evidence to support this theory of course; indeed in the very nature of the development as suggested above it is difficult to see how there could be. Nevertheless it seems to be tenable and it would certainly account for the apparent loss so early of a significant type of vessel.

The hoy, from the Dutch *heude*, appears in English records towards the end of the 15th century. It had the simplest of rigs, which consisted a little later of two sails only: a triangular headsail and a fore and aft mainsail, and these, with a single variation in the manner of rigging the mainsail, remained the hoy rig until it finally disappeared from use in the middle of the 19th century. Our information concerning the rig comes from inventories in the Admiralty records, dated 1536-1537.

The hoy was single-masted, as we might expect from our knowledge of the same vessel in the 17th century, and the mainsail was rigged with a sprit. This is quite different from the spritsail previously discussed – the square sail under the bowsprit. The sprit on the hoy was a spar which had its lower end lashed to the mast near the deck or with its heel against the foot of the mast on the deck. When the sail was set the sprit was diagonal to the mast, its upper end supporting the head of the mainsail, which was quadrilateral in shape (see p.58). The sprit thus had the function of the gaff, which in fact generally superseded the former towards the end of the 17th century. As there was only the one mast, the headsail had to be triangular and set from a stay. As it happens the smaller sail is not mentioned either as headsail or staysail, but there is little reason to doubt its existence, because sails – in the plural – are listed in one inventory whilst in the others 'the grete sayle' and 'the maynesaile' are specifically entered rather than just 'the sail' as might be expected if there were only one.

It is not clear whether the headsail was set to a stay in the bows or on a bowsprit. At this period the latter seems likely as in one of the inventories a bowsprit is listed and also because the hoy was still a relatively recent addition to English shipping and it seems probable that Dutch practices were still being followed. By the 17th century English hoys did not generally rig a bowsprit – although it would very much depend upon the whim of the master – whilst Dutch hoys continued to do so for another two hundred years.

In the 16th century hoys were commonly of less than 100 tons although there are records of these vessels at least twice that size. In the 17th century the

Herring busses, *c* 1650, R.Nooms, called Zeeman, 1623?– 1667. This illustration of a Dutch herring fleet at work shows the shape of the buss's hull. Practice while fishing obviously varied, some skippers electing to lower both fore and main masts out of the way, others content to leave the foremast rigged. The mizzen sail was left set to maintain tension on the long drift net that lay out to windward of the buss and was assisted by the windage on the hull as it was blown to leeward.

By this time – mid-17th century – it is clear that some buss skippers had forsaken the original square mizzen sail for a lateen sail.

average size increased because more of the very large type were being built. Despite this, however, the hoy was most often of between about 25 tons and 70–80 tons. Capacious, sturdily built and economical in rig and manning for their day, they were truly maids of all work. They were employed as coasters and short sea traders as well as being used as lighters from the early 16th century. They were employed as passenger vessels and yachts, when the use of the latter became fashionable in the late 17th century, whilst the navy used them extensively to carry stores of all kinds including powder and water.

Finally, to the number of these small vessels used as lighters we should add two or three regional craft. The keels of Norfolk or the Humber, and the trows of the River Severn occur in the records from medieval times. The fact that for some reason these craft tended to retain the single squaresail long after more efficient rigs were known and might have been introduced may suggest that this basic rig was that originally used. This may be, but unfortunately the records of the 15th and 16th centuries give us no clue at all.

These are only a few of the numerous types of vessel that served English trade during the period under consideration. The list probably includes the most important if as criteria for importance one considers the span of time covered by a type, *e.g.* the hoy, or in the case of the rather more obscure, the frequency with which they appear in the records.

The splendid work of John Hawkins and the likes of Matthew Baker notwithstanding, the most inventive of the maritime nations during this period was Holland. The first in the line of capacious seaworthy vessels produced by the Dutch was the herring buss in 1415, the year of Agincourt. As with most other vessels of that time there is very little evidence of hull form or rig and to have any idea of their appearance we must project backwards from what we know of the buss at a later date.

In the 16th and 17th centuries the herring buss had a high length-to-beam ratio rather in excess of 4:1, although it is most unlikely that these proportions, extreme for their day, were used in the 15th century. One should add however that we do not

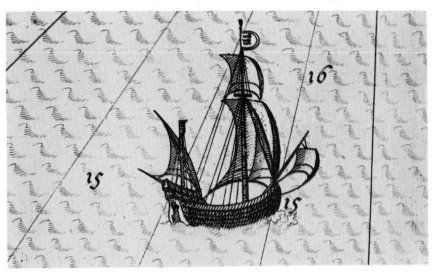

A *boier*, *c* 1586, Lucas Janz Waghenaer. This little drawing on a 16th century chart must be one of the earliest illustrations of a fore staysail on a deep-sea vessel. The artist either misinterpreted his notes or did not understand what he saw as the sails on the lower foremast are nonsensical as shown. Nevertheless, there is clearly a staysail set.

really know. Until the end of the 16th century the buss probably had a square stern and, if it followed the normal Dutch shipbuilding practice, a considerable tumble-home at the sides. The rig was three-masted with a square sail on each mast. Whilst fishing, the fore and mainmasts were lowered on to a gallows designed for the purpose near the stern; the small square mizzen sail was set to maintain tension on the net cable.

The herring buss evolved to enable a larger net to be worked and also to allow fishing in more distant waters. The unusual length of the buss provided the power for the former and, with its bluff bows and flat floors, the capacity for the storage of the salt in which the herring were packed in cask, and the additional stores necessary for a voyage beyond coastal waters. The buss would indeed be quite large and in the middle of the 16th century could carry home well over 200 tons of fish. Thereafter, however, perhaps because of the considerable investment involved and the consequent need to have a full hold to make a profit, the load of the average buss decreased to about 100 tons. Because their design for the far distant fishery made them good carriers, in the 16th century busses were used as cargo ships during the off-season for fishing. This has been suggested as one reason why the buss became so large and also why its size was reduced, which may have been the result of the development of a specialised cargo carrier, the *buyscarveel*. By their widespread use of the herring buss and the great net, and supported by efficient marketing, the Dutch came to dominate the herring industry.

They were not quite so successful in the cod fishery, although towards the end of the 15th century a special form of fishing boat was developed, the *hoeker*. These vessels had a special section of the hold amidships with a continuous watertight bulkhead at each end to protect the remainder of the ship.

The hull in this midships section was pierced with small holes to allow the free passage of sea water, and into the *bun*, as it was called, was placed the filleted cod soon after the nets had been emptied. By this means the fish was kept fresh until the return to harbour. Although doubtless rather sluggish in handling, a ship with a *bun* was as stable and seaworthy as one without. The *hoeker* is an excellent example of the ingenuity of the Dutch in creating specialised vessels; with a *bun* of course the ship could not be used for other purposes. *Hoekers* were in widespread use throughout the 16th and 17th centuries and many, in general carrying work, were built without the *bun*.

It was in the development of another particular type of vessel—although one by no means as narrowly specialised as the *hoeker* with the *bun*—that Dutch shipbuilders made their greatest impact in the 16th and 17th centuries. During that period the Dutch virtually made the bulk-carrying trade their own with the probable exception of the Baltic timber trade. In the *buyscarveel*, *boier*, *vlieboot* and *fluyt* one form of bulk-carrier followed another, each an improvement on its predecessor.

The line may have begun with the herring buss in fact, for it will be remembered that in the off-season busses were used as cargo vessels, trading as far as Spain. It will be remembered too that its capacity was one of the characteristics of the buss that enhanced its importance in the distant water fisheries in the North Sea and off the coast of Scotland. This theory is supported by the suggestion that the *buyscarveel* was basically a fully-decked buss with a low bow and rigged in the manner common in three-masted ships of the day: square spritsail under the bowsprit, square sails (course and topsail) on the fore and main masts and lateen mizzen (Richard Unger, *Dutch Shipbuilding before 1800*). The *buyscarveel* was introduced *c* 1550, which as we have seen was about the time that the buss declined in use as an off-season cargo-carrier.

Soon after the *buyscarveel* came the *boier*, widely in use by 1575. Although there is little contemporary evidence for the hull shape of the 16th century *boier* there are excellent drawings by the younger Willem van de Velde a hundred years later which illustrate the *boier* of his day (see p.58). The early *boiers* varied from 50 tons to 130 tons. Those of about 100 tons were most common with dimensions of roughly 65 ft in length and a little under 20 ft in beam. Two-masted with a form of early ketch-rig (*i.e.* main and mizzen masts as opposed to fore and main) the *boier* had a square spritsail, course and square topsail on the main, with a lateen mizzen. In one little sketch in Lucas Janz Wagenhaar's *Spiegel der Zeevaerdt* published in Leiden in 1586 what seems to be a *boier* is rigged with a fore staysail although the fact that the artist shows the main course set billowing out ahead of it suggests that his notes were not too accurate and that he certainly did not understand the rigging of sailing vessels. Assuming the information to be correct and only the artist's interpretation at fault, this must be one of the earliest depictions of a triangular headsail in use aboard a deep-sea vessel.

When discussing rig there are a number of points that should be remembered. First, that when we speak of a vessel rigged in such and such a fashion, we usually mean that this was the norm, the rig most commonly used for that type. We certainly cannot say that the rig of any particular type of vessel was immutably so. The rig was what the master said it was, and he would vary from the norm according to his own whims and prejudices. Second, in merchant sail an important factor in the modification of rig, not necessarily an improvement in pure sailing terms, was often the number of men required to handle it. Once a certain standard of sailing ability had been reached there was little or no incentive to increase it,

particularly if the modified rig would require more hands, because the only increase worthwhile to the owner was one that would enable the vessel to make an additional voyage in a season. Unless this could be achieved there was no profit in improved sailing and indeed it would almost certainly bring a reduced profit if more hands were needed. Consequently one usually finds that modifications were introduced into a rig in order to decrease the number of men in the crew and so maximise profits. Such modifications of course never led to a vessel making fewer voyages in a season. In warships the whole philosophy was different. The very existence of the ship might in action depend upon the speed with which her sails could be handled. Ships' companies were always therefore much larger than would have been profitable in a merchant vessel of a similar size, and the rig was occasionally different for the same sort of reason.

The *boier* was widely replaced in the 1590s by the *vlieboot* (English fly-boat). This bulk-carrier took its name from the region of the Vlie in northern Holland and was distinguished from the *boier* by its shallow draught. Not perhaps an improved version of the *boier* so much as an independent development out of the buss, the *vlieboot* had a high square stern and was broad in the beam. Like the *boier* the *vlieboot* had a two-masted rig that would have denoted a ketch later in the 17th century, with a square spritsail, course and topsail on the main mast and with a square topsail above the lateen mizzen. Although transatlantic passages were made in them, the *vlieboot* was largely used in the coastwise trade and, not surprisingly in view of its shallow draught, was normally fairly small in size, usually less than 100 tons.

However, in about 1600, the *vlieboot* itself was superseded in many bulk-carrying trades by the major achievement of Dutch ship design, which was to have an enormous influence on shipbuilding, particularly in England: the *fluyt*.

First Rate and Fluyt, 1600-1700

The 17th century was a period in which the innovations of 1560-1600 were confirmed and improved upon in their turn, although not, in some cases, without first having taken a half-pace backward. It was as if the shipbuilders of the day were not entirely convinced that measures forced upon them by the threat of war and proven in its execution were worth employing in times of peace. It was not therefore until the middle of the century that the principles established by Hawkins and Baker were taken up again to see how they could be developed further.

One problem to which attention was given quite early in the 17th century was that of steering the increasingly large ships that were then being built. Ever since the introduction of the centre-line rudder, probably in the 13th century, ships had been steered by means of a tiller, a horizontal lever in the fore-and-aft line of the ship attached to the rudder head. In fine weather the smaller vessels, *e.g.* the pinnaces of our period, could be steered directly by the tiller as in the modern dinghy, although with more difficulty of course. In heavier weather the helmsman needed the assistance of relieving tackles and other hands. In all larger vessels relieving tackles were probably required all the time. It must also be remembered that unless the vessel was well balanced, *i.e.* with masts properly placed, an appropriate sail plan, with the correct combination of sails set, and in addition a proper trim which usually required her to be slightly deeper in the water at the stern than at the bow, in any real weather she would virtually be unsteerable. Conversely, when all these factors were correct and the ship was on her best point of sailing, she virtually would steer herself in good weather.

Flemish galleon, 1593. This contemporary model in the Museo Navale in Madrid demonstrates the way in which the English galleons were copied after having proved their superior sailing qualities against the Armada in 1588. Particularly interesting is the spritsail topmast with its yard and furled sail, probably the earliest evidence of that rig.

The ability to steer a ship well—both in terms of the helmsman and of the means at his disposal—became increasingly critical the closer to the wind the desired course. If the ship's head was turned too close to the wind she was literally taken aback because the wind had come on to the wrong side of the sail (the forward side in the case of a squaresail) and was now trying to push the ship backwards. For several reasons this was to be avoided, principally because of the tremendous strain suddenly thrown upon rigging that had previously been slack and bearing no weight. Such a shock might well carry away a topmast or worse and imperil the ship in bad weather or on a lee shore. It must also be remembered the whole principle of supporting the masts was based on the premise that the thrust would be a forward pressure. Sails were of course deliberately backed in the performance of certain manoeuvres, but only under carefully controlled circumstances. If the vessel did jibe she would at the very least, not only lose speed and probably stop, but worse, she would drift to leeward and lose ground relative to the wind that could only be made up by a series of additional 'boards' or legs, in tacking. It will be seen then that as long as ships had to be steered by so imprecise and laborious a means as hauling on ropes led through a series of blocks, the ship's potential to sail close to the wind could not be realised fully for fear of accidents. When beating to windward, in fact, the helmsman had to steer some additional way off the wind, perhaps by rather more than a whole point ($11\frac{1}{4}°$), to allow sufficient margin for error. Another disadvantage of the relieving tackles method, which contributed to its lack of precision and immediate response, was the inability of the helmsman to see either ahead, or the sails and the difficulty of communicating with anyone who could. The tiller was on the gundeck. Above it on the larger vessels was at least one more deck and in some cases the wardroom on the quarter

deck as well. Communication was never easy. Instant communication was impossible. The first real attempt to solve these problems came with the introduction of the whipstaff.

This was an ingenious means by which one or two men could control the tiller of the largest ship in fine and moderate weather. Once it began to blow relieving tackles had to be used, but until then, with this more immediately responsive mechanism, the ship could be more precisely steered and so sail closer to the wind with reasonable safety. The arrangement of the whipstaff was simple (see illustration p.48). The bottom of a heavy pole, usually made of ash, was fastened to the forward end of the tiller and projected through a hole in the deckhead to the deck above. At the deck level it passed through a greased leather washer or grommet called the rowle, which permitted the whipstaff to pivot inside it and also slide up and down, whilst at the same time fitting round it snugly to prevent an excess of play. The helmsman stood on the deck above and by pushing the whipstaff handle to one side or the other could move the tiller below in the opposite direction. However, as the whipstaff moved in a plane perpendicular to that of the tiller—i.e. the tiller was moving in a lateral arc whilst the whipstaff end was swinging in a vertical arc—the latter had to be pushed downwards to compensate.

The whipstaff proved to be only an improvement on the previous method in some ships and at some times. It was certainly not a solution to the problem. It was an improvement in the smaller ships where the helmsman's position was immediately below the main deck. In those vessels he usually stood on a platform with his head in an open-fronted cupola. The latter was, one suspects, less to shelter him from the elements than to protect him from injury by careless movement on the deck above. Through the front of the cupola or hood he could at least see the sails and

The Return of the Dutch East India Fleet to Amsterdam, 1599, Andries van Eertvelt 1577–1652. The safe return from the Indies was always an occasion for rejoicing. In this case it was especially so as this was only the second fleet to make the round voyage. After 15 months, four of the eight ships in the fleet of the Far Lands Company of Amsterdam returned home. 'So long as Holland has been Holland,' said one contemporary observer, 'such richly laden ships have never been seen.' When the remaining four ships arrived in Amsterdam the return on capital for the investor exceeded 400 per cent.

The artist shows the big merchant ships riding high out of the water. The vessel under forecourse and maintopsail on the right seems to be one of the larger pinnaces.

gauge his course off the wind. He could also hear instructions from the officer of the watch for changes of course, or directions when in confined or crowded waters. He could not see ahead of the ship at all.

In larger ships the problem of communication remained. In the three deckers that became the first-class fighting ship from the middle of the 17th century onwards the space above the helmsman's head was enclosed as the wardroom. The nearest access to the open deck was some twenty feet or so forward of the whipstaff either up a ladder or else through the gratings which formed the upper deck there. Even in

two deckers there was a growing tendency to enclose the upper deck to just forward of the mizzen mast. It was this problem of communication one suspects, rather than the limitations of the mechanics of the whipstaff, which prevented ships being sailed as close to the wind as their potential allowed. It is true that they were not yet rigged with the fore-and-aft headsails that would enable them to sail close to the wind but these sails were consequent upon the solution of the steering problem rather precipitating it. We are here referring particularly to the fore staysail and the jib, the value of which had long since been appreciated on smaller vessels, but until the margin of error necessary for the helmsman could be drastically reduced there seems to have been little incentive to rig them on major vessels. That at least is the inference from later events, for within two or three years of the steering problem being solved by the introduction of the wheel *c*1703, jibs and staysails were fitted in accordance with Admiralty Instructions and other nations rapidly followed suit.

It may have been an unconscious groping towards the same solution to the problem that had led the northern nations to adopt the spritsail topsail early in the 17th century at much the same time that they brought the whipstaff into general use. Spanish documents show the whipstaff to have been in use in the 1560s, forty years earlier than has hitherto been supposed. Its use was probably uncommon at that date, however, or one would expect to find at least a reference to it in Dutch or English records. Perhaps Hawkins did not know of it, although that might be considered surprising in view of the intelligence networks of the day and the general interchange of knowledge about ships. If it was known in England it was certainly not used in English ships until about the time the spritsail topsail was introduced. Nor can we be certain who was responsible for the introduction to northern waters of these two fittings.

If, as has been suggested above, they were brought together with the idea that with better control of the bows, greater advantage could be taken of the improved sailing qualities by an improved steering mechanism, the experiment was a failure. However, until something better could be devised the 'experiment' was persisted with for just about 100 years. Set from a yard on the spritsail topmast which was rigged in the top at the extreme end of the bowsprit, the spritsail topsail was some 30ft above the water and so likely to pick up bouncing wind currents that would miss the spritsail; for the same reason, it would not tend to become filled with water as could the spritsail. At the same time it is difficult to see how the spritsail topsail would be of great help in sailing by the wind, although set so far forward it would certainly exert considerable leverage useful in manoeuvring. On the other hand, that same forward position could also tend to exert leverage downwards, thrusting the bows deeper into the water to the detriment of her sailing qualities. Not enough is known about the positive qualities of the spritsail topsail, nor of exactly how and when it was used to the best advantage. Whatever those qualities were, they must have been worth having and they must have outweighed the disadvantages, or the mast and its yard and sail would not have lasted for 100 years. As to its relevance to the whipstaff, the similarities are sufficient in number to cast doubt upon their being entirely coincidental. First there is the timing: introduced by the northern nations at the same time that they adopted the whipstaff, both were discarded in the early years of the 18th century. Second, there is the parallel with the wheel and triangular headsails, a similar experiment that was highly successful. Third, both were used only in big vessels. Fourth and finally, each was used only in fair weather, the sail not used in bad weather, the spritsail topmast often being struck, whilst under such conditions, although the whipstaff was still rigged, the work of controlling the tiller was done by relieving tackles.

There is no record of either the ship or the date in which the whipstaff and the spritsail topsail were first used in the Royal Navy but it seems most probable that it was in the first years of the 17th century. As both were easily added to any existing vessel they may first have appeared in the several 'rebuilds' and the one or two newly built warships of the 1590s. The term 'rebuilt' seems to have been used fairly indiscriminately, perhaps for political purposes, for work done on a vessel from a 'great repair' to the literal rebuilding of one that had been taken to pieces. Usually, in a rebuild there was an element of the

original ship involved in the way of serviceable timbers that could be used again. The whipstaff and spritsail topsail were, naturally, also put in the newly built and rebuilt ships of the new reign.

These ships, including the new *Repulse* and *Warspite* of 1596, were not built under the same strict control as had been the practice in the 1580s. Hawkins had died at sea in 1595 and by 1604 not only had the careful, even parsimonious, reign of Elizabeth ended, but the finances of the navy had passed into the hands of Sir Robert Mansell, who, though a creditable seaman, proved to be probably the most corrupt official of the 17th century. We are not concerned with Mansell's faults here except that they indicate a laxity in control; a laxity which soon showed itself in the newly built ships.

Efficient sailers that Hawkins's ships were, they must undoubtedly have been less comfortable for the officers than their predecessors, simply because of the reduction of the upperworks aft where the officers were quartered. It was natural therefore that as the

The Return of the Prince of Wales from Spain, 1623, Hendrik Cornelisz Vroom 1566–1640. The flagship *Prince Royal* leads in (from right to left) *St Andrew, Defiance, Swiftsure* all built for the Navy Board Commission 1618–1623 by William Burrell. As it is October, the ships are in their winter rig with no spritsail topmast rigged, no topgallants and no topmast on either of the mizzen masts.

memory of the great threat from Spain became dimmed and the strict control of Hawkins was removed, the senior officers would look to their comfort and prestige. As a result, by the early years of the 17th century the superstructure aft was again increasing in height as great cabins were made larger and deckheads higher. It is not clear whether English ships were the leaders in this trend or merely followers of fashion. Certainly other nations had copied the sleeker lines of the Elizabethan galleons of 1588, and certainly Dutch ships of 1599 were high in the poop.

Constant Reformation, 1619, Willem van de Velde (the Elder), 1611-1693. One of the first ships built for the navy by William Burrell, the *Constant Reformation* was lost at sea in 1651. With a keel of 106 ft, beam 35½ ft and a depth in hold of 15 ft she was of 752 tons (ton and tonnage, roughly equivalent to modern gross tonnage). Originally designed to mount 42 guns, in the later stages of her career, as depicted here, she carried some 62 guns. The step in the lower gun deck aft is clearly indicated by the position of the guns.

Into this category one might almost put the *Prince Royal* built by Phineas Pett in 1610, except that she was so large – by far the greatest ship of her time – that her cabins could be roomy and still not have the somewhat top-heavy appearance of other ships of James I's reign (see p.44). Nevertheless she proved crank (*i.e.* a poor sailer) and decayed rapidly, having been built with green, unseasoned timber. The *Prince Royal* was used to carry Princess Elizabeth to Flushing in 1613 and for Prince Charles's voyage to Spain in 1623, after an expensive refit and repair costing £20 000. She saw no sea-service thereafter and was completely rebuilt in 1641, an instance of the name being almost the only part of the original ship being used again. However, the concept was correct even though it was spoiled by Pett's cupidity. She carried 55 guns on three decks, and with a keel

of 115 ft and a beam of 43 ft was almost twice the tonnage of either the *Ark Royal* or the *Victory* of Elizabeth's reign.

As a result of the Navy Board's corruption and negligence from 1603–1618, the office was put into Commission which lasted for ten years. During the first five years ten new ships were built which, if they did have rather higher superstructure aft than would have pleased Hawkins, did yeoman service for many years. For example, in the eight years for which the accounts are available between 1638 and 1652, three of the ten averaged nearly 300 days at sea per year whilst four more averaged well over 100 days. The longest lived, the *St. George*, is last mentioned as a hulk in 1697, 75 years after her launching. Some of these vessels still carried the fourth mast, but the painting by Vroom suggests that the decision may have been left to individual captains, for the *St. Andrew* is rigged with three masts. The bonaventure mizzen was not used after the 1620s.

In rigging, the natural step forward was taken and a topgallant sail was added to the foremast; square topsails were also rigged on the mizzen and bonaventure-mizzen masts.

An interesting addition to the navy in the last year of the Commission (1627) was a class of ten small cruisers called whelps. They were not given names but were numbered 1–10 instead; their 'class' name came from a similar vessel, the *Lion's Whelp*, bought from the Lord Admiral (the Earl of Nottingham) in 1601. They were the first class of vessels to be built to the same design, although two of them differed slightly in size from the remainder. Unfortunately there is no original illustration of them but we know that the eight similar whelps measured 62 ft on the keel with a 25 ft beam, giving a gross tonnage of 185 tons. They each carried 14 guns and were intended to hunt the Dunkirk privateers that preyed upon the Channel trade.

The most famous warship of the 17th century, the *Sovereign of the Seas*, was completed in 1637. The masterpiece of Phineas Pett, she seems to have suffered from his predilection for the grandiose as had the *Prince Royal* a generation earlier. Splendid in concept as she was, she too was not a good sailer until some of her upperworks were either removed or lowered in 1651. She was built with a keel length of 127 ft and a beam of 46 ft 6 ins and was the first ship to bear 100 guns (in the sense of being heavy ordnance) and the first to have three continuous decks without falls. This force was considerably greater than any other vessel afloat in her day and in that and her rig she can claim to be the true forerunner of the great ships of the line of the 18th and 19th centuries. However, she was a poor sailer and a 100 guns are of little account if they cannot be brought into action at the right time. The *Sovereign of the Seas* was completely rebuilt in 1660 and that *Sovereign* rebuilt again in 1680.

The *Sovereign* of 1637 brought two innovations in rig: royal sails were set above the topgallants on both fore and main masts and a topgallant sail was set above the mizzen topsail. The royals cannot have been a success for there seems to be no suggestion that they were repeated in either 1660 or 1680, and they were not fitted as standard rig for another 150 years.

By the early years of the 17th century, English shipbuilders had established a considerable reputation as builders of defensible ships—*i.e.* ships that were armed. This had no doubt developed from the events of 1588 and the domination, by threat at least, of the northern waters outside the Baltic during the remainder of Elizabeth's reign. English ships were renowned for their strength and their sea-keeping qualities as well as for their guns and their crews, and were sought after even by the Venetians in 1618 in preference to Flemish vessels that were actually cheaper. For all that, however, Flemish and Dunkirk ships most frequently appear to be the best sailers in the first half of the century, with the Dutch next and English vessels a long way behind. There was little to choose between them in rig and not much difference in the quality of seamanship. English ships were undoubtedly more heavily built and sat deeper in the water than their Dutch counterparts, for the coast of Holland demanded vessels of relatively shallow draught. Whilst this would undoubtedly have affected the sailing qualities, there was no great disparity in that regard between the English and Dutch ships in the First Dutch War (1652–1654), yet neither country was building ships appreciably differently than they had been earlier. The records suggest that the difference in say the 1620s was largely a matter of how often the ships were breamed. This entailed careening the ship, *i.e.* hauling her over on to one

side after beaching her, so that at low water the marine growth could be burned and scraped off. It was common practice for the Dutch to bream their vessels every two months and at the same time treat the planking below the waterline with tallow. The English navy's practice was to bream about every three months, usually without the application of tallow afterwards to inhibit new growth.

The difference between the bottoms was demonstrated in a devastating and humiliating manner in 1623. The *Garland*, under Captain Thomas Best, and the *Bonaventure*, both ships newly-built by the commissioners, were sent to convoy back to Ostend a Dunkirker which had been blockaded in Leith harbour by Dutch men-of-war. On the way south however, the Dunkirker could not resist the temptation to show off his superior vessel, and suddenly crowding on all sail he left both English and Dutch

The *Sovereign of the Seas*, 1637, J.Payne, *c* 1607–1647. This splendid contemporary portrait shows the royal yards on the fore and main masts with furled sails, and also the furled topgallant sail on the mizzen. The *Sovereign of the Seas* was the first vessel on which these sails were rigged. The long low beakhead was soon to disappear, and the profile of the remainder of the hull set the fashion for sailing warships for the next hundred and fifty years. Compare the profile with that of the *Prince Royal* and her consorts on p.44. All the decks open to the weather were covered by an additional 'grating deck' on which people are seen standing.

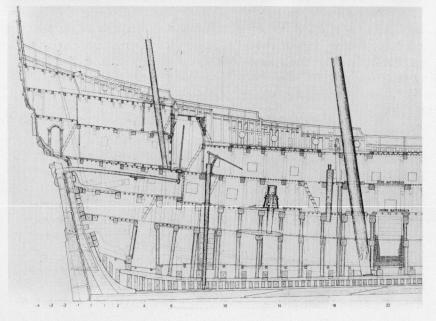

Wasa, 1628. The photographs above show (left) the upper deck viewed from the beakhead looking aft. The catheads to which the anchors were secured immediately after weighing project forward at an angle over the beakhead rails which curve inward below them. (right) The view along the gun deck shows well the massive timbers used in the construction of a large wooden ship. Light and air reached the lower decks principally by means of the hatches, which were protected by removable gratings. Right forward can be seen the heavy bitts which took the strain of the anchor cable.

(below left) The inboard works from the mainmast to the stern. The whipstaff is just forward of the mizzen mast and forward of that again a pump reaching down almost to the keel. Notice the size of the timbers and the many centreline pillars in the hold and the orlop above it. Below decks the timbers in outline are the great riders, 12–18 inches square, which reinforced the frames and planking.

ships standing, shortening sail again only when he was nearly two miles ahead. Unfortunately for him the Dutch squadron also outsailed Best's ships and took full advantage of the time gained by pouring a broadside into the Dunkirker, bringing down her main yard and killing the captain and five of the crew. The Dutch withdrew as the English vessels arrived on the scene, leaving the chastened privateer to her escort. However, the four Dutch ships continued in company, amusing themselves and infuriating the hapless Captain Best by sailing around the little convoy in wide circles until it came to anchor in the Downs.

By the time of the First Dutch War, in which by coincidence both the *Garland* and the *Bonaventure* were lost, there is no suggestion of such a difference, for the new brooms among the Commonwealth's administrators had once again rejuvenated the service in both its *matériel* and its organisation.

As we have seen, Dutch ships were shallow in draught. It was not the same with warships of either Denmark or Sweden, which were built more in the English style, heavy in construction and deep in the water. In 1628 a great new flagship, the *Wasa* named after the Swedish royal house, capsized and sank dramatically in Stockholm harbour as she put to sea for the first time. The fault, a combination of miscalculation and poor judgment, resulted in gun ports already too close to the water being left open on the lee side as the ship heeled to a stiff breeze. The *Wasa*'s position was lost after some initial attempt at salvage and she was not rediscovered until 1956. She was recovered surprisingly intact in 1961 and now lies in the Wasa Museum, Stockholm (see illustrations p.48).

By the second half of the 17th century the major warship had settled upon lines that were to be only marginally changed for the next 200 years. There were minor differences in design between the ships of the Royal Navy and those of the continental powers, especially those of Holland and France, the latter following the re-establishment of a soundly based navy by Colbert between 1662 and 1683. The long low beakhead was replaced by a shorter, wider version set at a higher angle to ship less water in heavy weather. France and Holland continued to use the square-tuck stern whereas English ships had a round tuck, *i.e.* the planking below the main wale continued round to the stern post. English and French ships tended to have less sheer, giving a straighter line to the silhouette; both these countries developed three-deckers although there was a tendency to mount fewer guns in French ships of similar dimensions; this, together with their generally greater beam provided a more stable gun platform. The Dutch did not build three-deckers until towards the end of the century, when they were not completely successful, probably because of the constraints of requiring a shallow draught. Dutch vessels also retained a more marked sheer. Both French and Dutch favoured more tumble-home—the inward curve of the ship's side to reduce weight above the waterline and improve stability.

We have seen that additional sails were introduced early in the century. The process continued as main and mizzen staysails were added, together with main and fore topmast staysail in the 1680s, all of which improved performance to windward. As ships became larger there was a need in warships to increase the sail area. The courses were already almost at the maximum size that could be handled efficiently, but main and fore topsails were increased. Their greater size however made it imperative that the area could be reduced when the wind increased, whilst still leaving sufficient sail that could be effective. Bonnets were never very practical on topsails and so, in the early 1660s, reef points were reintroduced so that the topsail could be shortened by gathering part of it up

Resolution in a gale, 1669, Willem van de Velde (the Younger), 1633–1707. This splendid painting shows a Third Rate with shortened sail in heavy weather. The topgallant masts have been sent down to reduce weight and windage aloft, and all the topsails are furled.

The courses are not reefed and the yards appear to have been lowered, which suggests that this incident took place just before reefing was reintroduced. The bonnets have been removed and the yards lowered to improve stability.

to the yard above and securing it there by the reef ties.

The middle of the 17th century also saw, for English ships at least, the final break between warships and merchant vessels. After the First Dutch War no merchant ship was hired to stand in the battle line as had been the case previously. In future only warships as such were used. Merchant ships of certain types continued to carry ordnance for another century or more in trades and waters where they might be subject to piracy or action from ships of a rival nation. By contrast the Dutch navy persevered with armed merchants ships in their fleet for rather longer although they had pioneered the development of the unarmed merchant ship especially designed for its trade. Perversely, from the Dutch point of view, this was to have a considerable effect on the development of English ships and shipbuilding later in the century.

Before looking at the mainstream of commercial shipping in the 17th century we should consider some of the smaller craft which, although of little significance in their day, paved the way for a future development in rig or vessel type. Most of the Dutch vessels that we have so far considered remained in use during this period and longer. Throughout the whole of the century there were *busses, hoekers, vlieboots* and *heuden*; some of them appear in English records later in the century with anglicised names such as hookers, flyboats and hoys. It is not clear however, to what extent these latter names refer to English versions of Dutch craft. With the exception of the hoy, which was well established in England in the 16th century, it seems probable that they were Dutch-built vessels bought as prizes of war.

Many of the other small craft of the 17th century were rigged with some form of fore-and-aft sail. Most commonly it was the spritsail, which in some cases needed quite a heavy spar as vessels like the hoy, for example, increased in size. Perhaps because of this, by the middle years of the century an alternative fore-and-aft sail had been developed in an early form of the gaffsail. In this, the large sail that the spritsail had become was held up by a long gaff often called a half-sprit. Its derivation from the spritsail may also be seen in that the sail had no boom; instead it was furled by brailing in to the mast. Another form of the gaffsail, already in common use in Holland in the 1630s, when it would seem that the half-sprit was only just coming into use, was the short-gaff sail. This was a long sail much narrower at the head than the foot – hence the name – and consequently it is unlikely that it owed anything of its origin to the spritsail. It was not brailed but could be lowered to the deck.

These sails in combination with the fore staysail and square sails, formed the rig of a number of craft which developed in the 17th century. We must be a little chary of using names which since the 19th century have assumed a particular meaning. It will be convenient to do so however provided that we record the period each time referring, for example, to a 17th century sloop. The name was in common usage for most of the 17th century and is defined and illustrated in the middle of the next so that it seems reasonable to hazard a guess that until the emergence of the gaffsail in either of its forms, a 17th century sloop was rigged with a spritsail and a fore staysail; after about 1660, when it was commonly found on yachts, sloop rig seems to have consisted of gaffsail and forestaysail.

The term 'ketch' was also in widespread use in England during the 17th century. Like the galiot and the *hoeker* it was two-masted with a tall main mast and a short mizzen mast. All three were probably rigged with a combination of sails from the following: fore staysail, course and square topsail and a gaff or lateen-rigged mizzen. Towards the end of the century a new type of warship was introduced by the French, a *galiote à bombes*. As adopted by the Royal Navy it was usually ketch-rigged, but not invariably so. The ketch rig was suited to the vessel because it enabled the main mast to be stepped well aft to allow the heavy mortar a clear field of fire forward.

Also towards the end of the 17th century we find the first mention of the term 'brigantine'. Illustrations show this as a vessel with a fore and main mast, with course and topsail on the fore, and short-gaff mainsail with a square topsail. Other illustrations from the early 18th century show this rig with a long-gaff mainsail but whether it had been in use 30 years earlier is problematical. At this period of course, and for long after, no distinction was made between 'brigantine' and 'brig' for the terms were accepted as synonymous.

A Zealand ship at anchor, Abraham Willaerts *c* 1603-1669. This painting demonstrates clearly the standard rig for a major warship of the mid-17th century. Beneath the bowsprit is the square spritsail, above is the spritsail topsail. Fore and main masts have course, topsail and topgallant; above the lateen mizzen is a square topsail. The cro'jack yard is rigged just below the top and was chiefly used to secure the tacks of the topsail. The cro'jack, a sort of mizzen course was rarely used and is not bent on to the yard in the picture. The standing rigging, *i.e.* that which supports masts and does not move, is well drawn. On this Dutch vessel the beakhead is angled upwards more than was the English practice (see p.47).

In the 17th century we also find the first indications of the schooner rig. Illustrations dated earlier than mid-century show small Dutch vessels with fore and main masts, each bearing a short-gaff sail. In one drawing dated *c*1650, although there is a boom on each sail, the foresail is clearly loose-footed. On none of these early schooner-rigged yachts, however, is there a fore staysail. The earliest illustrations showing a staysail with this rig could hardly be dated much before 1700 (and with boomless sails) but in view of the wide use of the fore staysail on other rigs during the last decades of the century it would be reasonable to guess that the schooner had them too.

Although the early yachts (Dutch *jacht*) both Dutch and English are associated with the 17th century, the type clearly had its origins at least in the 16th century, for by 1600 it was used for a multitude of purposes, involving state, government, commerce or pleasure, but always with the desire for speed in mind. Early in the century yachts commonly had the spritsail sloop rig of the period but by the 1630s this had given way to the short-gaff sail. The *bezaanjacht* introduced at about this time had a jib and a fore staysail, gaff mainsail and occasionally a square topsail above it.

For many years it has been assumed that yachting in England began with the Restoration of the monarchy in 1660, and indeed that the word was really introduced into the language at the same time. However, the household accounts for Hurstmonceux

Hoys in a fresh breeze, *c*1685, Willem van de Velde (the Younger). This drawing demonstrates the use of the half-sprit or long-gaff sail which replaced the spritsail in the mid-17th century. On the right the brails are seen, slack and lying across the sail; on the left they have been hauled in to brail the sail to the mast. Both gaff sails, the long which was brailed in or the short which was easily lowered to the deck, were much simpler to hand (*i.e.* take in) and set than the spritsail with its heavy sprit-boom.

Hoy at anchor, *c*1686, Willem van de Velde (the Younger). This handsome little vessel shows all the characteristics of a small Dutch hoy: long bowsprit, standing (or long) gaff and round stern. The leeboards were used as drop keels and, pivoted at the forward end, were lowered on the lee side when under way to reduce drift to leeward. Like the centreline drop keels of the late 18th century, they were of particular value in shallow waters. This hoy, riding high in the water, is obviously empty.

Castle in Sussex for the year 1643-1644 contain several references to 'my lord's yaught' which was kept at Pevensey. Unfortunately there is no indication as to its rig and little to show its size, except that it was large enough to have a dock built for it. English yachts of the 1660s were often copies of Dutch vessels, but they soon attained their own characteristics, discarding the shallow draught necessary in Dutch waters and assuming the design and appearance of small warships. Most of the numerous royal yachts of the later Stuarts did in fact serve the navy in varied and most useful ways. After 1682 when another Pett built *Fubbs* for Charles II, nearly all English royal yachts were ketch-rigged, although some were given the three-masted ship rig when serving with the navy.

A contemporary Dutch writer of the time states that the first *fluyt* was built in 1595 at Hoorn and that ten such ships were built there annually for the next eight years (Unger). Whether that is true or not, we do know that the *fluyt* was introduced at about the turn of the century and was immediately successful. Initially designed with a length to beam ratio of 4:1, the proportions were increased in the first decade or so to 6:1. The *fluyt* was designed to carry the maximum amount of cargo and consequently was given the largest possible hold below her single deck. This was achieved by a stem and sternpost that were almost vertical, with full lines and flat floors for much of her midships length. Forward there were virtually no upperworks but aft there was a narrow poop above a round stern (see p.32). The first *fluyts* were probably little larger than the *boiers*, about 150 tons, but they were quickly increased in size to vary between about 200 tons and something less than 500 tons. In 1670 an average *fluyt* had an overall length of about 120ft and a beam of 22ft. Their success was based on maximising the profit margin and it typifies the pre-eminence of Holland in building and operating merchant ships for most of the 17th century. Organised capital made it easy for would-be owners to borrow funds and for enterprising builders to build speculatively. The ships were well designed for their particular trade. In the case of the *fluyt* the construction was relatively light, for without ordnance the ship had no need to withstand either the weight of the guns or the shock of their discharge. Nor, since there would be no occasion to fight, need she be strong enough to withstand gunfire; all of which meant a cheaper vessel, relatively quickly built. Once at sea her lack of height forward reduced windage and made her easier to control, whilst her considerable length and good run aft, a product of the round stern, made her a reasonable sailer considering her general hull form. Her rig was kept simple: square spritsail, fore course, main course and topsail, lateen mizzen and square topsail. The masts were often rather short for the length of keel, and sails were generally smaller than those on a warship or defensible merchant ship of similar size for ease of handling in order to keep the number of crew to a minimum; topsails were sometimes dispensed with entirely for similar reasons. At the same time the ship suffered little loss in efficiency because with her relatively light construction she had no need to be heavily canvassed.

As early as 1605 Sir Walter Raleigh reported that the ratio of tons carried per man of crew was 20:1 on Dutch ships by comparison with a ratio for English ships of 7:1. It is impossible to check Raleigh's figures, but tables for comparable vessels in the mid-18th century produced by Ralph Davis (*The Rise of the English Shipping Industry*), makes them seem probable enough. In the same work Professor Davis shows that even by 1686 English vessels entering London from Spain and Portugal, the West Indies and the American colonies had still not reached a level of 9 tons per man.

During the first 30 years or so of the 17th century the *fluyt* was adapted to a number of specialised trades. Originally conceived as a bulk carrier, and indeed the role in which it was most widely used, with bluff bows and slightly heavier construction the *fluyt* became a major carrier in the timber trade of the Baltic and the coal trade from the north-east coast of England. With a specially strengthened bow for use among ice floes, the *fluyt* became a whaler; still another version known as a *katschip* was produced in the form of the Scandinavian cat vessel, the characteristics of which were a simple straight stem without a beakhead, bluff bows and a narrowing stern. Above all the cat had pole masts with no tops, so that yards could be lowered to deck level and no man need go aloft when working the sails, hence a further reduction in manning. The pole masts, of course, were the chief feature distinguishing the *katschip* from other *fluyts*. An interesting variation in rig is that the *katschip* had a gaff-rigged mizzen instead of a lateen, probably the first ship of any size to do so.

A smaller and probably unrelated ship also acted as a jack-of-all-trades: the galiot. This two-masted vessel had a gaff-rigged mainsail and a lateen mizzen, with the greatest beam forward of the main mast.

Used extensively in the coastal trade it was used for fishing as well as for carrying passengers and general goods. The Dutch East India Company (Vereenigde Oost-Indische Compagnie or VOC) also used galiots as despatch vessels in their service to the Far East.

The VOC ships were two-decked defensible vessels of the type pressed into the battle line by Holland in wartime. They were not unlike their counterparts in the English Honourable East India Company in that generally during the 17th century they remained about 400–500 tons. In 1610 HEIC launched the *Trades Increase*, a huge ship for her day, of 1100 tons. Unfortunately she was lost in 1613 on her first voyage, the members of the company learning the hard way that giant vessels were as much at hazard as ships half their size, whilst the financial risk was twice as great. Thereafter smaller ships were built to reduce the risk of crippling loss and it was nearly 200 years before either country produced merchant ships of a thousand tons. The West Indiamen also remained at about the 200–300 ton mark. It should be remembered that although these were all defensible ships their hull lines were by no means as fine as those of warships; nor were they as full in the body as the cats and *fluyts* of the bulk trades.

Two *fluyts* adapted for their trade, *c* 1650, *Ooster-vaerder* and *Noorts-vaerder*, Zeeman 1623?–1667. In warships, tumble home aided stability by lowering the centre of gravity. In merchant vessels, whilst the same advantage obviously accrued, the real reason was often more commercially based. Tolls in the Sound (between Sjaelland and the Swedish mainland) were based upon beam at the weather deck level; consequently ships with tumble home paid appreciably lower tolls than would have been levied had they been wall sided.

On the left of the illustration, the Baltic trader of her day, the *Ooster-vaerder*, has a pronounced tumble home. The *Noorts-vaerder* on the other hand, built for the Norwegian timber trade, has much less.

We saw that at the beginning of the century the Dutch, having concentrated on the development of economical carriers, had not only assumed the dominance in the northern trade that had previously been largely in the hands of the Hanseatic League but in addition dominated the North Sea fisheries as well. England, on the other hand, had made herself a maritime power by building a large and efficient navy. It was inevitable that as English merchants and shipowners sought to expand their trade throughout the world, the two nations would clash.

There were numerous and continuous reasons for the antipathy felt on each side. English merchants and shipowners were angry about the preponderance of foreign vessels, largely Dutch, in the coal trade between Newcastle and London; there was rivalry on the fishing grounds of the North Sea and in the whale fishery off Spitzbergen; the Dutch were continually affronted by English demands that their ships should strike their topmasts and dip their en-

A Whaling fleet in the ice, Abraham van Salm, *fl* 1700. This grisaille drawing shows typical merchant ships at the end of the 17th century. Whaling ships differed little from those in other trades except that their bows were strengthened for work among ice floes. Two interesting features are the settee sail instead of the triangular lateen sail set on the ship on the left, and the small two-masted vessel in the centre which has a fore staysail, a long-gaff mainsail and a short-gaff mizzen.

signs to English warships in the Channel; most vehement of all was the hatred after the massacre at Amboina in 1623, an attempt to discourage the HEIC from trading in the Far East. Despite these often bitter differences, war between England and Holland was postponed because the tension was eased with the latter's involvement in the European wars from the early 1620s until 1648. During these years Dutch trade declined and England's trade increased—in the West Indies, the American colonies, the Far East, the eastern Mediterranean. In the Newfoundland fishery alone 250–300 ships sailed from England each year. It is not surprising then that Anglo-Dutch rivalry should be sharply rekindled when the latter began to win back a share of the lost trade in the first years of peace the Dutch had known for a quarter of a century.

England's immediate response was the passing of the Navigation Acts of 1651 which banned the unloading of goods in English ports unless they were in English ships or those of the country in which the goods originated. The First Dutch War broke out the following year. Indirectly it solved England's shipping problems and ensured her eventual ascendancy over the Dutch.

The key factor lay in the 1200–1500 (estimates vary) prizes taken from the Dutch between 1652 and 1654, most of which were *fluyts* and all of which, by nature of their origin, were good cargo carriers. These ships were sold quite cheaply to English owners who immediately benefited from their capabilities, particularly those ship owners trading from the north-east. Two other Dutch Wars followed, conveniently spaced (1665–1667 and 1672–1674), and although neither produced so rich a haul as the First Dutch War, sufficient prizes were taken to ensure a reasonable supply of these valuable vessels as the first were beginning to wear out. By the time the Dutch-built ships needed replacing with others newly-built

in English yards, the owners had been profiting by their particular virtues for some 30 years, and they were understandably reluctant to return to the ill-suited defensible ships the English yards offered.

English shipbuilding was at that time concentrated on the Thames and the East Anglian ports of Aldeburgh, Ipswich, Woodbridge and Yarmouth. The builders however were unwilling to change their techniques and, it seems, refused to build the type of vessel the owners wanted. There is unfortunately no documentary evidence that this happened but the facts certainly support the argument first put forward by Professor Ralph Davis. In the last years of the 17th century the former shipbuilding centres in East Anglia declined, never really to recover. At the same time the requirements of the shipowners were met from English yards somewhere and by the middle of the next century shipyards on the north-east coast had a considerable reputation for building that same type of ship; all of which suggests that the few yards already in existence at such places as Whitby and Scarborough, close to the area that had most need of bulk-carrying vessels, seized their opportunity with both hands and were joined by others with an eye to the future. The vessels produced were not slavish copies of the *fluyt* but a larger adaptation of it, with all the same qualities, which became known in England as the North Country cat. It probably did not however have the pole masts of the Scandinavian cat-built ships. Unfortunately, no direct record of these vessels in their early years has survived. From the requirements of the bulk-carrying trade, and the vessels in that trade in the middle years of the 18th century for which there is information, these ships were simply but sturdily built, plain and unadorned to keep costs to a minimum. They had bluff bows and flat floors to maximise the stowage space and also to allow them to take the ground safely. They were probably fitted with the standard rig of the closing years of the 17th century: square spritsail, course and topsail on the fore and main masts, and lateen mizzen with a square topsail. It is unlikely that they carried a spritsail topmast.

During the 16th century, the lumbering and un-handy three-masted ship that had been developed a hundred and fifty years earlier was made into a manoeuvrable and seaworthy vessel needing just one further sophistication, an adequate method of steer-ing to enable it to reach the limits of its development. In the 17th century, as we have seen, the necessary steering control eluded the innovators despite useful steps in the right direction. Instead, the 100 years which followed the death of Queen Elizabeth saw the evolution of the 'big' ship in its two main forms: as a ship of great force, capable of carrying a hundred guns into action and also as a ship of great profit, built cheaply and operated economically, carrying the most cargo possible on a given keel length worked by the minimum number of men. At the same time experience of the fore-and-aft sail not only presaged the arrival in the next century of the last major innovation in sailing ship design, the schooner, but also, in its introduction as staysails, enhanced the capability of large ships in sailing on a wind. The story of the final step, the combination of wheel and triangular headsails—the first allowing control of the tiller ropes from a point on the upper deck where the helmsman could see the sails and be within earshot of the officer on deck, the second allowing the ship to be steered much closer to the wind with safety—is one for the first years of the 18th century.

An English cat, c 1700, Willem van de Velde (the Younger), 1633-1707. This drawing conveys the shape of the North Country cat well and may have been one of the early *fluyt*-type vessels built on the north-east coast.

57

Bibliography

Anderson, Romola and R.C. *The Sailing Ship*, (New York, 1963).

Boxer, C.R. *The Portuguese Seaborne Empire*, (London, 1969).

Burwash, Dorothy *English Merchant Shipping*, (Toronto, 1947).

Davis, Ralph *The Rise of the English Shipping Industry*, (London, 1962).

Greenhill, Basil *The Archaeology of the Boat*, (London, 1976).

Landstrom, Bjorn *The Ship*, (London, 1961).

Lane, F.C. *Venetian Ships and Shipbuilders of the Renaissance*, (Baltimore, 1934).

McGrail, Sean *Rafts, Boats and Ships* (*The Ship book 1*), (London, 1981).

Martinez-Hidalgo, José *Columbus' Ships*, (Barre, Mass., 1966).

Moreton-Nance, R. Numerous articles in *Mariner's Mirror*.

Oppenheim, M. *History of the Administration of the Royal Navy*, (London, 1896).

Unger, R.W. *Dutch Shipbuilding before 1800*, (Amsterdam, 1978).

Waters, D.W. and Naish, G.P.B. *The Elizabethan Navy and the Armada of Spain*, (NMM monograph no.17, 1975).

Boier, c 1675, Willem van de Velde (the Younger), 1633–1707. This delightful drawing gives some indication of the size reached by this sprit in the mid-17th century and the reason for the development of the long gaff.

The original form of the *boier* (see p.37) had virtually disappeared by c 1650, and the name was being used to describe the fore-and-aft rigged, round-sterned vessel seen here.

Index

6/11/87   39.95 (10 vol. set)   Barnes/Noble 14469

THE SHIP

All titles in *The Ship* series are available from:
HER MAJESTY'S STATIONERY OFFICE

Government Bookshops

49 High Holborn, London WC1V 6HB
13a Castle Street, Edinburgh EH2 3AR
41 The Hayes, Cardiff CF1 1JW
Brazennose Street, Manchester M60 8AS
Southey House, Wine Street, Bristol BS1 2BQ
258 Broad Street, Birmingham B1 2HE
80 Chichester Street, Belfast BT1 4JY

*Government publications are also
available through booksellers*

The full range of Museum publications
is displayed and sold at
National Maritime Museum
Greenwich

**HMSO
BOOKS**

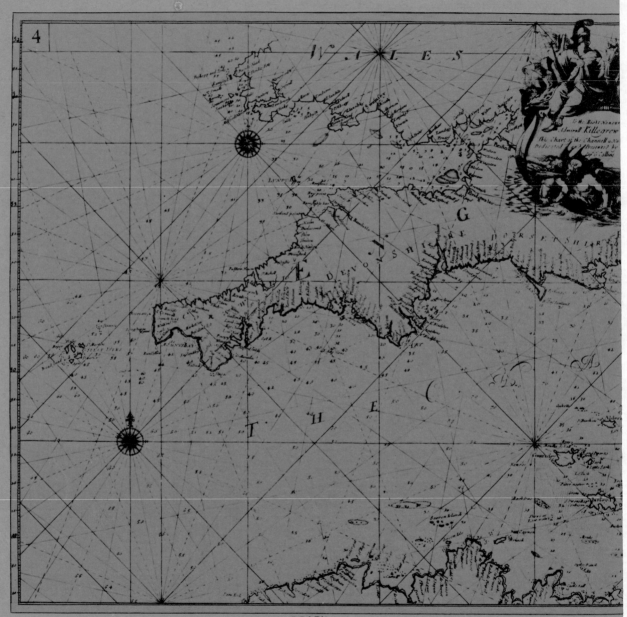